REPENT & BELIEVE

LOVING GOD WITH ALL YOUR HEART

Discipleship Training for Small Groups

Repent & Believe: Loving God with All Your Heart

Devoted: Discipleship Training for Small Groups

Copyright © 2020 by Clear Creek Community Church and Aaron Lutz

Editorial Team: Mandy Turner, Ryan Lehtinen, Jon Coffey

Published by Clear Creek Resources

A Ministry of Clear Creek Community Church

999 North FM 270

League City, Texas 77573

ISBN: 978-0-9979469-6-3

Unless otherwise indicated, all Scripture quotations are taken from:

The Holy Bible: English Standard Version, copyright © 2001 by Crossway Bibles, a division of Good News Publishers. Used by permission. All rights reserved.

All Scripture emphases have been added by the authors.

Printed in the United States of America

CONTENTS

INTRODUCTION

What are you repenting of? What are you believing to be true as you follow Jesus?

This study marks the halfway point of the Devoted: Discipleship Training for Small Groups series. By now we've gained more than a familiarity with the Spiritual Growth Grid and its three gospel storylines—hopefully it has become the lens through which we see and interpret the truth of God's word in our lives and challenge others to do the same.

In Year One, we began with Jesus's call to repent and believe in the gospel: Now after John was arrested, Jesus came into Galilee, proclaiming the gospel of God, and saying, "The time is fulfilled, and the kingdom of God is at hand; repent and believe in the gospel" (Mark 1:14-15).

But Jesus isn't speaking here about a one-time repentance or simply an initial belief in the gospel. Remember Martin Luther's famous line: "When our Lord and Master Jesus Christ said 'Repent,' he intended that the entire life of believers should be repentance." So, what are you repenting of? What are you believing to be true as you follow Jesus?

On the surface, those questions might sound like an exercise in great effort. When we rely on God (the impetus of last year's Repent and Believe study), we begin to practice obedience—living by the Spirit, rather than our flesh, and submitting ourselves to a disciplined lifestyle focused on walking in God's power.

But, as we begin Year Two, I want to remind you that the choice to Repent & Believe is not only an act of laying down an old way of living but also turning toward a joyful, intimate, thrilling love relationship with the God of the universe. There is nothing more exciting than being found at the center of God's will—which includes this call to Repent and Believe.

This study will focus on loving God with all your heart. We pray that these 9 weeks would not just be a practice in stimulating your intellect but would deeply stir your affections for Jesus. Our hope is not that you would know more about God, but that you might love him more deeply. We pray that you are inspired to love, perhaps in a new way, and that this love would transform you to look more and more like Christ, more and more like the image of God. And we pray that, as a result, you would reflect God's kind of love to those who are far from him—that you'd be a disciple who makes disciples. That is the purpose behind the Devoted series.

Grace to you,
The Elders of Clear Creek Community Church

USING THE STUDY

Devoted is a two-year small group study series focused on training in the essentials of being a disciple who makes disciples. It is designed to help small groups grow deeper in the concepts of the Spiritual Growth Grid. This means, regardless of where you are on the spiritual journey, you play your part in the group each week when you:

Step 1: Memorize the Scripture

Throughout the study you will memorize key Bible passages specifically chosen for the topic. Practice reciting these each day. Try to fill in the blank spaces from memory as you prepare to recite the passages at your next small group meeting.

Step 2: Study the Scripture

The Bible passages are chosen because of the study's general theme. They are good Scriptures to know as either citizens, family, or missionaries. They don't necessarily relate directly to the day's teaching. This is a section where we want disciples to grow in the skill of observing and interpreting a text. The teaching that follows will deal with biblical application.

Step 3: Read the Teaching

Take your time to read through the day's teaching. The questions that follow are designed to help you better process the lesson in light of the Spiritual Growth Grid and apply the principles. Afterwards, take time to pray using the prompts provided.

Step 4: Do the Weekly Exercise

You will find a weekly exercise at the end of each week's Day 3 material. The exercises often employ different learning styles to practice the principles been taught. Be sure to not only do the exercise but the reflection section as well. The exercises are intended to help build your skill set as a disciple-making disciple.

Step 5: Ready Yourself for Group

The last section of each week's material concludes with the *Get Ready for Group* section. This allows you to summarize your key takeaways for the week in preparation for small group discussion. Please be sure to answer the final question concerning how the week's lessons help you better integrate the Spiritual Growth Grid. This will help your Navigator identify possible areas of further study in order to better live out one's gospel identity. Remember, the point is to be trained to be a disciple who makes disciples!

01

WHOLEHEARTED DEVOTION

SCRIPTURE MEMORY

Hear, O Israel: The Lord our God, the Lord is one. You shall love the Lord your God with all your heart and with all your soul and with all your might.

—Deuteronomy 6:4-5

COMMANDS AND BLESSINGS FROM THE GARDEN

Scripture Study

GENESIS 1:27-31

So God created man in his own image, in the image of God he created him; male and female he created them.

28And God blessed them. And God said to them, "Be fruitful and multiply and fill the earth and subdue it, and have dominion over the fish of the sea and over the birds of the heavens and over every living thing that moves on the earth." 29And God said, "Behold, I have given you every plant yielding seed that is on the face of all the earth, and every tree with seed in its fruit. You shall have them for food. 30And to every beast of the earth and to every bird of the heavens and to everything that creeps on the earth, everything that has the breath of life, I have given every green plant for food." And it was so. 31And God saw everything that he had made, and behold, it was very good. And there was evening and there was morning, the sixth day.

Observing the Text

Make a list of the actions God takes towards humanity. Note the repetition of certain verbs.

_____

_____

_____

What are the commands God gives the first man and woman? Do any of these verbs seem to be synonyms?

_____

_____

_____

Interpreting the Text

What does this passage demonstrate about the character of God?

_____

_____

_____

Why does it matter that God blessed them before he commanded them to do anything? What is God's desired outcome for humanity in this text?

_____

_____

_____

Teaching

"In the beginning God created…"

The first two chapters of Genesis probably get more air time than any other passage in the Old Testament, not only because God created, but because of *who* he created and *why* he created. There is a foundational nature to the text that draws us in; it is our origin story. We love Genesis 1-2 because God is answering some of our deepest philosophical questions:

> *Who am I?*
> *Why do I exist?*
> *Why is there something instead of nothing?*

We may also be drawn to this passage because sin hasn't ruined everything yet. We get a two-chapter glimpse into what life was like in God's kingdom without the stain of sin all over it. God creates to reflect his own glory. Think about that. The stars in the sky, the water and land, the plants and animals—in their purest forms, every aspect of creation reveals the undeniable preeminence of God. The things that God has made lead us to worship their maker. What an incredible gift!

Humanity is the climax of that creation. We were lovingly made in the image of God, not only to reflect his likeness, his righteousness, and holiness (like Ephesians 4:24 describes), but also to know him, worship him, and love him. Bearing God's image isn't simply a call to be holy because God is holy, it's a call to love because God is *love* (1 John 4:8). Love isn't just something God does, it's something he is.

In the creation narrative, only humanity is given the remarkable dignity and worthiness to bear the image of God. The rocks don't have the privilege of knowing God in an intimate relationship. The seas may roar, but they don't experience the joy of worshipping God and being known by Him. The stars don't know what it means to love or be loved. But God created humanity with a unique capacity for relationship as a reflection of his own character. Wholehearted devotion to God has always been God's plan for mankind.

God created us in love and joy, welcoming humanity into an eternal relationship between the Father, the Son, and the Holy Spirit. He didn't create out of loneliness or need—God is fully known and fully loved in the Trinity—but out of a desire to extend that intimate love to a wider circle, to humanity. And then God blessed us, pronouncing special favor on the people he had made. He declared the pinnacle of his creation to be very good.

He blessed human beings. Then, in the same breath with this blessing, he gave the first imperatives, or commands. Notice that the first commandment wasn't "Don't eat the fruit of that tree." God's first directives were to be fruitful and multiply, and to subdue the earth and have dominion over it. Unlike what we may sometimes assume, these commands aren't given in response to, or anticipation of, disobedience. The commandments of God weren't given to be burdensome, they were part of the blessing.

Often, when we approach Scripture (especially the Old Testament), we interpret God's imperatives as oppressively onerous, because we often have a broken view of how authority should work. Sin has stained how we see anyone or anything that tries to tell us how to live our lives. But, these commands were given from a loving and holy God, before the Fall, as part of the blessing of God on humanity. You could even argue that the command in Genesis 2:16-17 to not eat of the tree of the knowledge of good and evil was part of this same blessing, couched in the context of our loving creator calling us into a relationship of wholehearted devotion to him.

God didn't command Adam and Eve in order to control them; he commanded them in order to fulfill the purpose of his creation; to reflect his glory, to know him intimately, to worship him fully, and to deeply experience his love. Why? Because he knew that this was best for them. Before sin ever entered the picture, God commanded obedience, and his desire was that man would respond in love—wholehearted devotion to him. God created us to be image bearers, finite beings called to mirror the goodness of an infinite God. We exist to glorify God and enjoy him forever.[1] Thus, God's plan from the beginning was that man would know and be known by God, experiencing his love and responding with a whole-hearted devotion to him.

As we consider what it means to repent and believe, we must recognize that God's imperatives are an act of love, and he longs for our response to move toward him.

Questions for Reflection

In what ways is humanity designed to reflect the image of God? How can you, as a finite being, affected by sin, reflect the goodness of an infinite, holy God?

_____

_____

_____

What imperatives has God given in Scripture that you often see as burdensome, but are in fact part of the blessing intended to call you to deeper devotion to God?

_____

_____

_____

---

1 Westminster Shorter Catechism. http://shortercatechism.com/resources/wsc/wsc_001.html

How might God be calling you to repent of an old way of viewing his commands and believe more fully in the gospel? What does that repentance look like practically?

_____

_____

_____

Prayer

Imagine life before sin entered the picture. Picture God as Father, Son, and Holy Spirit—fully known and fully loved, welcoming you into that relationship. Thank God for creating you. Express your love and gratitude to Jesus. Ask the Holy Spirit to allow you to see God's commands as an act of love and respond in obedience this week.

SCRIPTURE MEMORY

Hear, O_____: The Lord our God,
the Lord is one. You shall_____the
Lord your God with all your heart
and with all your soul and with all
your might.

—Deuteronomy 6:4-5

COMMANDS AND PROMISES FROM UR

Scripture Study

GENESIS 1:27-31

So God created man in his own image, in the image of God he created him; male and female he created them.

28And God blessed them. And God said to them, "Be fruitful and multiply and fill the earth and subdue it, and have dominion over the fish of the sea and over the birds of the heavens and over every living thing that moves on the earth." 29And God said, "Behold, I have given you every plant yielding seed that is on the face of all the earth, and every tree with seed in its fruit. You shall have them for food. 30And to every beast of the earth and to every bird of the heavens and to everything that creeps on the earth, everything that has the breath of life, I have given every green plant for food." And it was so. 31And God saw everything that he had made, and behold, it was very good. And there was evening and there was morning, the sixth day.

GENESIS 22:15-18

And the angel of the Lord called to Abraham a second time from heaven

¹⁶and said, "By myself I have sworn, declares the Lord, because you have done this and have not withheld your son, your only son, ¹⁷I will surely bless you, and I will surely multiply your offspring as the stars of heaven and as the sand that is on the seashore. And your offspring shall possess the gate of his enemies, ¹⁸and in your offspring shall all the nations of the earth be blessed, because you have obeyed my voice."

Observing the text

How many times in these two selections from Genesis does God use the word bless or blessing? Circle them in the reading above. How would you define blessing in your own words?

_____

_____

_____

What commands does God give Abraham in Genesis 12 and Genesis 22? How does Abraham respond?

_____

_____

_____

What promises were made to Abraham?

_____

_____

_____

Interpreting the text

Were God's blessings dependent on Abraham's obedience? Why does this matter?

_____

_____

_____

What does it mean that they "regarded Christ according to the flesh," but no longer do?

_____

_____

_____

What do these blessings/promises say about God's character?

_____

_____

_____

Teaching

Imagine living a relatively comfortable lifestyle in your hometown. You have friends and family close, you have a great job, and all your needs are met. Life is good. But then, imagine God makes it clear that it's time to leave—to move somewhere you don't know anyone, without a certain job lined up, or clarity on how you'll pay the bills once you get there.

That is where we find Abraham in Genesis 12.
To leave Ur of the Chaldeans—to leave his father's house—would be to leave the only security he'd ever known.

But God spoke.

And, Abraham listened.

In fact, before this moment, Abraham didn't even know this God who was speaking to Him. Abraham was a worshipper of false gods (Joshua 24:2). But Abraham heard a new voice speak a compelling command to go, and he chose to obey. Why?

Hebrews 11:8 gives us some insight: *"By faith Abraham obeyed when he was called..."*

Initially, Abraham didn't obey out of certainty, or obligation, or even out of love, yet. Abraham obeyed by faith. To have faith simply means to trust— to believe something of which you are not yet certain. So, what did Abraham trust? Did he trust God's voice, believing that he had a duty to obey the command? Or did he trust that God's call to follow must be connected to the promises God was making? Notice, the command in Genesis 12 is coupled with some pretty outstanding promises. In the same breath where God commands Abraham to go, he promises to make him into a great nation, meaning God would give him a family. Abraham's barren wife would have a child. Even though Abraham and his wife were past their child-bearing years, God was promising to build them into a great family, and through that family, bless the entire world.

God wanted Abraham to obey, not out of obligation, but by faith—not by focusing on the command but being captivated by the promise.[1] Throughout the rest of the Bible, Abraham is celebrated not for his good works, but for his faith.

In Genesis 22, this faith is put to the test. Abraham is asked to sacrifice his only son, Isaac. Abraham's faith is on display in an intense scene on a mountain in Moriah, where he binds Isaac and raises a knife to slay his son. But even in this moment, Abraham doesn't question God's goodness or his faithfulness. He has already decided to trust in the promises of God— by faith. How and when God will provide might be unclear, but Abraham trusts in the promises of God.

---

1 Steve Fuller, "God's Gracious Path to Costly Obedience," Desiring God (June 2013) https://www.desiringgod.org/articles/gods-gracious-path-to-costly-obedience.

On Day 1, we learned that God's commands are often coupled with a blessing. Imperatives aren't a curse or oppressive in nature, they are a blessing from God intended to lead us to wholehearted devotion to him. Today, as we consider what it means to live a life of repentance and belief, we must repent of treating God's commands as an obligation or duty. Rather, we must see the beauty within the promises God makes when we listen and obey his commands. What some may read as a list of rules, statutes, and commands in Scripture, those who live by faith recognize them as being connected to a greater promise. Abraham obeyed because he was captivated by the promises of God.

Are you captivated by the promises of God?
Are you captivated by the gospel?

When I (Aaron) first met my wife and started to get to know her, I was captivated by her presence. I wanted to spend more and more time with her, and the more I got to know her, the more mesmerized and enthralled I became. Nothing else in the world mattered. I was captivated, and it changed how I lived, how I loved, and how I prioritized my time.

Are you captivated by the gospel?
Has it changed how you live and love and spend your time?

Notice the promise in John 3:16: "For God so loved the world, that he gave his only Son, that whoever believes in him should not perish but have eternal life."

That's a promise.

But notice, this promise comes not as a result of our obedience, but as a result of Jesus's obedience in our place.

When Abraham, by faith, was willing to sacrifice his only son, God provided a lamb to die as a substitute for Isaac. In the gospel, God provides his only son to die as a substitute for us. Jesus is the Lamb of God who died to take on the sins of the world. When given the choice, Jesus obeyed the Father and laid down his life for you, because he was captivated by the promise: that we could know God and be known by him, that we could love God and be loved by him, that our relationship with him could be restored.

When we are captivated by that gospel, the commands of God are no longer rules to follow, but an opportunity to express our wholehearted devotion to God. Part of repenting and believing the gospel is being captivated by the goodness of God.

Questions for Reflection

What other commands in Scripture are connected to a promise?

_____

_____

_____

What most often motivates you to obey God—duty, obligation, fear, reward, love? How does faith in the promises of God change your motivation?

_____

_____

_____

How does the gospel change the way you view God's commands in Scripture?

_____

_____

_____

Prayer

Be silent for a few minutes. Let the Holy Spirit remind you of your life before Jesus. Then, express your joy in the gospel. Tell God why you love him and why you needed Jesus's obedience in your place. Commit today to be captivated by the gospel.

SCRIPTURE MEMORY

Hear, O Israel: The Lord our God, the Lord is one. You shall love the Lord your God with all your_____ and with all your_____and with all your_____.

—*Deuteronomy 6:4-5*

COMMANDS AND A
WEDDING IN THE DESERT

Scripture Study

EXODUS 20:1-21

And God spoke all these words, saying,

2"I am the Lord your God, who brought you out of the land of Egypt, out of the house of slavery.

3"You shall have no other gods before me.

4"You shall not make for yourself a carved image, or any likeness of anything that is in heaven above, or that is in the earth beneath, or that is in the water under the earth. 5You shall not bow down to them or serve them, for I the Lord your God am a jealous God, visiting the iniquity of the fathers on the children to the third and the fourth generation of those who hate me, 6but showing steadfast love to thousands of those who love me and keep my commandments.

7"You shall not take the name of the Lord your God in vain, for the Lord will not hold him guiltless who takes his name in vain.

8"Remember the Sabbath day, to keep it holy. 9Six days you shall labor, and do all your work, 10but the seventh day is a Sabbath to the Lord your God. On it you shall not do any work, you, or your son, or your daughter, your male servant, or your female servant, or your livestock, or the sojourner who is within your gates. ¹¹For in six days the Lord made heaven and earth, the sea, and all that is in them, and rested on the seventh day. Therefore the Lord blessed the Sabbath day and made it holy.

¹²"Honor your father and your mother, that your days may be long in the land that the Lord your God is giving you.

¹³"You shall not murder.

¹⁴"You shall not commit adultery.

¹⁵"You shall not steal.

¹⁶"You shall not bear false witness against your neighbor.

¹⁷"You shall not covet your neighbor's house; you shall not covet your neighbor's wife, or his male servant, or his female servant, or his ox, or his donkey, or anything that is your neighbor's."

¹⁸Now when all the people saw the thunder and the flashes of lightning and the sound of the trumpet and the mountain smoking, the people were afraid and trembled, and they stood far off ¹⁹and said to Moses, "You speak to us, and we will listen; but do not let God speak to us, lest we die." ²⁰Moses said to the people, "Do not fear, for God has come to test you, that the fear of him may be before you, that you may not sin." ²¹The people stood far off, while Moses drew near to the thick darkness where God was.

Observing the Text

What does God say before he gives the Ten Commandments? (v. 2) What actions does he take after the Ten Commandments are listed

_____

_____

_____

List the Ten Commandments in your own words. (v. 3-17) Which command is connected to a promise?

_____

_____

How did the people respond to these commands (v. 18-21)?

_____

_____

_____

Interpreting the Text

Why is it important for God to remind the Israelites both who He is and who they are? Why do you think God begins with identity statements?

_____

_____

_____

Compare and contrast the Israelites' response to God speaking with how Moses responds. (v. 18-21) Why did Moses draw near while the people drew back from God?

_____

_____

_____

Teaching

The book of Exodus begins with God hearing the cries of his people. God hears. God cares.

Several chapters later, he sets a plan in motion to rescue the people of Israel from their oppression and slavery in Egypt. He tells Moses to relay this message to his people:

> _"I am the LORD._
> _I will bring you out..._

I will deliver you...

I will redeem you...

I will take you to be my people, and I will be your God."

Exodus 6:6-7

God begins with an identity statement: "I am the LORD"—Yahweh, the covenant-making, promise-keeping God. Then, he describes his activity on their behalf, making four specific promises.

But, here is where it gets interesting. These four promises later become the same four promises a Jewish groom would make to his bride in an ancient Jewish wedding: I will bring you out, I will deliver you, I will redeem you, and you will be my people.[1] These promises become wedding language.

The Exodus story has always been seen as a covenant-making story. In the culture of the Ancient Near East, a king would establish his rule by clarifying his expectations for his kingdom, while also making promises to govern and protect. When God brings the nation of Israel to Sinai, they would have recognized that Yahweh, the king, was establishing a covenant relationship with his citizens.

But, some scholars in early rabbinical tradition began to interpret this story not only in terms of a king-citizen relationship, but they also saw God's actions as comparable to that of a husband. The Exodus account not only recounts a rescue story, but it illustrates a marriage-type relationship where God serves as the groom and Israel his bride. In fact, ancient Jewish wedding ceremonies were designed to recount this story in Exodus.

So, when you read Exodus, think about it this way: God, the groom, is bringing out his bride, delivering her, redeeming her, and preparing her

---

1 These are also the same four promises recounted in the four cups of the Passover celebration.

for relationship with him.

But, as we continue reading, we discover that the honeymoon was short-lived. God's chosen bride, Israel, grumbled and complained incessantly, ungrateful for the rescue. After 400 years in slavery, they found themselves in a desert, wondering how they would eat and survive. But Yahweh, with unending patience and compassion, responded by providing and protecting.

Exodus 13 tells us that God's presence hovered over them in the form of a cloud by day and fire by night. The Hebrew word for this is *shekinah*. The *shekinah* glory of God was meant to remind Israel that God had not abandoned them; he was leading them and would provide for them. His presence was over them.

For centuries, Jewish weddings have featured the groom and bride standing under a canopy-like prayer shawl stretched and affixed to poles known as a *chuppah* (pronounced HOO-pah). It symbolically represents God's presence over the wedding, just as the cloud of God's *shekinah* covered his people. The couple then, exchanges vows beneath the *chuppah* as God hovers over them, willing to protect and provide for this newlywed couple.

In Exodus 19, God told Israel to prepare themselves. Speaking again as a groom to his bride, Yahweh declared them to be his "treasured possession" and told them to consecrate themselves, because on the third day his presence would come down on Mount Sinai. When the day came, the people were ready to hear from God. Thunder. Lightning. A thick cloud covered the mountain, and Moses went up to meet with God.

God spoke.

And the result?

The Ten Commandments.

When we read the Ten Commandments, we don't often think about them in terms of romantic language. We often read this passage as a list of rules to follow, tasks we are required to accomplish, or activities that are forbidden to us.

However, the Ten Commandments were never meant to be seen this way. In the Jewish wedding ceremony, a couple signs a contract called the *ketubah*—a legally binding document that acknowledges their vows. They both affirm the work it will take to live as husband and wife, and then they sign the ketubah under the chuppah.

Israel saw the Ten Commandments as a *ketubah*—an agreement between Yahweh and his bride regarding their display of love for each other. Thus, the first commandment, to have "no other gods before me," is a commitment to faithfulness; it's an agreement that this relationship doesn't work if you have other lovers. A commitment to Sabbath rest establishes a trust in God, the groom's, provision. "Honor your father and mother" is a reminder of how the family of God relates to one another. The Ten Commandments were never meant to be a killjoy. They were vows made in accordance with how God's people might relate to a holy God.

The pattern we've seen in God's work of creation and his calling of Abraham continues in Exodus 20, and especially evident in the gospel of Jesus.

> Through Christ's work on the cross,
> he has brought you out,
> delivered you,
> redeemed you,
> and taken you as one of his own people.

So how do we respond to this kind of love?

Deuteronomy 6:4-5, our scripture memory for the week, calls us to love the Lord our God with all our heart, soul, and might. It's interesting to note, this text is just one chapter after Moses recounts the Ten Commandments in Deuteronomy 5. The anticipated response to the commands of God is a wholehearted devotion to him.

To love the Lord your God with all your heart, with all your soul, and all your might has been God's plan from the very beginning.

Questions for Reflection

Consider the Spiritual Growth Grid.

REPENT & BELIEVE			
WHO GOD IS	WHAT GOD DID	WHO WE ARE	WHAT WE DO
KING	CALLED	CITIZENS	LISTEN & OBEY
FATHER	ADOPTED	FAMILY	LOVE & SERVE
SAVIOR	SENT	MISSIONARIES	GO & MULTIPLY

Why is it significant that God establishes his identity before he makes the four promises (to bring out, deliver, redeem, take)?

_____

_____

_____

How does this teaching stir your affections for God? How does this cause you to love God more?

_____

_____

_____

What might change in our lives when we begin to see the commandments of God as deeply connected to the blessings, promises, and faithfulness of God?

_____

_____

_____

Prayer

Pray a prayer of repentance. Confess any ways that you treat God's law as a list of rules to follow, or perhaps ways you've tried to earn his love by keeping the commandments. Commit to believe in the gospel more fully, expressing your devotion to God at a heart level. Let the Holy Spirit stir your affections for him and a desire to obey, not out of obligation, but out of wholehearted devotion.

WEEKLY EXERCISE

LIFE MAP/HAND OF GOD MOMENTS

At Clear Creek Community Church, one of the tools we have adopted to help people share their story of faith is what we call a Life Map. It's a visual representation of one's life over time and the heroes (spiritual mentors) who played a part, the heritage (family of origin) that influences our stories, the high points and hard times, and finally, the hand of God moments. This last section is where we will spend some time today.

Where have you seen the hand of God show up in your life? Week 1 of this study intentionally traced some of the first moments in the history of God's people to show us an early account of God calling his people to full devotion through his commands. How have you seen God do the same thing your life? Looking back, what are some key moments where God was calling you to love him with all your heart, soul, and might?
Chart it using the table below.

Hand of God

The Early Years (Birth—)	The Next Years (—)	The Last Years (—)	The Now Years (—)

Get Ready for Group

Write your memorized Scripture.

_____

_____

_____

_____

_____

What observations and interpretations of Scripture were most meaningful
to you?

_____

_____

_____

_____

_____

Summarize your key takeaway(s) for this week.

_____

_____

_____

_____

_____

What will you tell the group about the results of your exercise this week?

_____

_____

_____

_____

_____

How has this week helped you better understand and apply the Spiritual Growth Grid?

_____

_____

_____

_____

_____

REPENT & BELIEVE

WHO GOD IS	WHAT GOD DID	WHO WE ARE	WHAT WE DO
KING	CALLED	CITIZENS	LISTEN & OBEY
FATHER	ADOPTED	FAMILY	LOVE & SERVE
SAVIOR	SENT	MISSIONARIES	GO & MULTIPLY

02

WHAT FEELS LIKE LOVE TO GOD

SCRIPTURE MEMORY

Hear, O Israel: The Lord our God, the Lord is one. You shall love the Lord your God with all your heart and with all your soul and with all your might.

—*Deuteronomy 6:4-5*

DAY
1

OBEDIENCE AND LOVE

Scripture Study

DEUTERONOMY 5:1-21

*And Moses summoned all Israel and said to them, "Hear, O Israel, the statutes and the rules that I speak in your hearing today, and you shall learn them and be careful to do them. ²The Lord our God made a covenant with us in Horeb. ³Not with our fathers did the Lord make this covenant, but with us, who are all of us here alive today. ⁴The Lord spoke with you face to face at the mountain, out of the midst of the fire, ⁵while I stood between the Lord and you at that time, to declare to you the word of the Lord. For you were afraid because of the fire, and you did not go up into the mountain. He said:
⁶"'I am the Lord your God, who brought you out of the land of Egypt, out of the house of slavery.*

⁷"'You shall have no other gods before me.

⁸"'You shall not make for yourself a carved image, or any likeness of anything that is in heaven above, or that is on the earth beneath, or that is in the water under the earth. ⁹You shall not bow down to them or serve them; for I the Lord your God am a jealous God, visiting the iniquity of the fathers on the children to the third and fourth generation of those who hate me, ¹⁰but showing steadfast love to thousands of those who love me and keep my commandments.

11"'You shall not take the name of the Lord your God in vain, for the Lord will not hold him guiltless who takes his name in vain.

12"'Observe the Sabbath day, to keep it holy, as the Lord your God commanded you. 13Six days you shall labor and do all your work, 14but the seventh day is a Sabbath to the Lord your God. On it you shall not do any work, you or your son or your daughter or your male servant or your female servant, or your ox or your donkey or any of your livestock, or the sojourner who is within your gates, that your male servant and your female servant may rest as well as you. 15You shall remember that you were a slave in the land of Egypt, and the Lord your God brought you out from there with a mighty hand and an outstretched arm. Therefore the Lord your God commanded you to keep the Sabbath day.

16"'Honor your father and your mother, as the Lord your God commanded you, that your days may be long, and that it may go well with you in the land that the Lord your God is giving you.

17"'You shall not murder.

18"'And you shall not commit adultery.

19"'And you shall not steal.

20"'And you shall not bear false witness against your neighbor.

21"'And you shall not covet your neighbor's wife. And you shall not desire your neighbor's house, his field, or his male servant, or his female servant, his ox, or his donkey, or anything that is your neighbor's.'

Observing the Text

Compare this reading of the Ten Commandments with the reading from Exodus 20. What differences do you see in how Moses relays the commands?

_____

_____

_____

List any identity statements God makes in this passage.

_____

_____

_____

Interpreting the Text

What does this passage say about the character of God?

_____

_____

_____

What can you discover about the context of this passage in the book of Deuteronomy? Why is Moses restating these commands at this point in Israel's history?

_____

_____

_____

Our scripture memory verse, Deuteronomy 6:4-5, comes one chapter after this recounting of the Ten Commandments. Why do you think this is significant?

_____

_____

_____

Teaching

Last week we began looking at the Ten Commandments with the purpose of understanding why God would set forth commandments in the first place. Wholehearted devotion was his plan from the very beginning.

This week we will consider the Ten Commandments from a different perspective: How does God receive love? What feels like love to God?

In 1995, Gary Chapman wrote a book called *The Five Love Languages: How to Express Heartfelt Commitment to your Mate*. Chapman, a pastor and Christian counselor, proposes the theory that everyone expresses and experiences love in one of five ways:

- Receiving gifts
- Quality time
- Words of affirmation
- Acts of service
- Physical touch

The thesis of the book is that each of us tend to express love to our partners in the way that we personally like to receive it. So, in order to discover your partner's love language, you must observe the way they love others, analyze what they complain most about, and detect patterns of how they prefer to be loved (or just take the online quiz). Chapman argues that trouble comes when one person's love language doesn't align with that of their partner. I may be a person who is affected most by words of affirmation, but my spouse might feel loved with acts of service.

So, take our relationship with God, which is intended to be a joyful, intimate, thrilling love relationship with the God of the universe. We may attempt to express love towards God in a way we think is appropriate, but still somehow miss how God receives love. How do we discover God's love language? Couldn't he just take the online quiz?[1]

Fortunately, God has already revealed to us how he prefers to receive love.

---

1 Note that God is not limited by the Five Love Languages in Chapman's book.

First, let's look at the numbers.

There are 613 commandments in the law. The Ten Commandments are just a fraction of them. There are 365 negative commands ("Do not...") and 248 positive ones ("Do..."). But, that's more than just Bible trivia. By looking at the numbers alone, we can feel the sheer weightiness of the law God gives.

That feeling should become even more overwhelming when we also consider these texts:

> *If you love me, you will keep my commandments.*
>
> John 14:15

> *For this is the love of God, that we keep his commandments. And his commandments are not burdensome.*
>
> 1 John 5:3

> *And this is love, that we walk according to his commandments...*
>
> 2 John 6

The love language is obvious, isn't it? If we really love God, we should seek to know and keep his commandments. He has made it even clearer than the results of an online quiz. If we are not keeping his commandments, if we choose to withhold obedience or reject repentance, can we honestly say we love God?

We may look the part, dress the part, talk the part. We may do good works or show up at a church service every week thinking this is how we please God, thinking this is how God receives love. But God makes it clear: he feels loved when we respond with obedience. A reliable means of measuring our love for God is to examine whether or not we listen and obey.

A helpful and important reminder needs to be said here, however. Pastor and author Kevin DeYoung reminds us that while our obedience is an expression of our love, it should never be seen as a means of earning God's love:

> Note once again that the law comes after gospel—after the good news of deliverance. God did not come to the people as slaves and say, "I have Ten Commandments. I want you to get these right. I'm going to come back in five years, and if you've gotten your life cleaned up, I'll set you free from Egypt." That's how some people view Christianity: God has rules, and if I follow the rules, God will love me and save me. That's not what happened in the story of the exodus. The Israelites were an oppressed people, and God said, "I hear your cry. I will save you because I love you. And when you are saved, free, and forgiven, I'm going to give you a new way to live."

> We need to hear it again: salvation is not the reward for obedience; salvation is the reason for obedience. Jesus does not say, "If you obey my commandments, I will love you." Instead, he first washes the feet of the disciples and then says, "If you love me, you will keep my commandments" (John 14:15). All of our doing is only because of what he has first done for us.[2]

The Ten Commandments are a reminder of who God is and how he receives love. May we respond to his sacrificial love with a love that sacrificially obeys him.

---

2 Kevin DeYoung, "Five Reasons to Obey the Ten Commandments." The Gospel Coalition (October 2018) https://www.thegospelcoalition.org/blogs/kevin-deyoung/five-reasons-obey-ten-commandments/

Questions for Reflection

In the past, how have you tried to please God? What are some ways that you are trying to please him now? How do your attempts compare to what you just read?

_____

_____

_____

Why is it important to recognize that God rescues Israel before he gives them the law? How does this relate to how we come to repent and believe in the gospel?

_____

_____

_____

The Ten Commandments are a reminder of who God is and how God receives love. What are a few commands he gives and what do those commands reveal about God's character? (e.g. Do not murder – God is the author of life.)

1. _____

_____

2. _____

_____

3. _____

_____

Prayer

Pray through the Ten Commandments, affirming your commitment to love God by keeping each of them. Ask God to reveal his character through these laws. Confess any area of sin that comes to mind.

SCRIPTURE MEMORY

Hear, O Israel: The_____,
the Lord is one. You shall_____
_____with all your heart
and with all your soul and with all
your might.

—Deuteronomy 6:4-5

THE LAW OF LOVE

Scripture Study

MATTHEW 22:34-40

But when the Pharisees heard that he had silenced the Sadducees, they gathered together. ³⁵And one of them, a lawyer, asked him a question to test him. ³⁶"Teacher, which is the great commandment in the Law?" ³⁷And he said to him, "You shall love the Lord your God with all your heart and with all your soul and with all your mind. ³⁸This is the great and first commandment. ³⁹And a second is like it: You shall love your neighbor as yourself. ⁴⁰On these two commandments depend all the Law and the Prophets."

Observing the text

What was the intent of the Pharisees and Sadducees by asking Jesus about the "great commandment in the Law"?

_____

_____

_____

Of the 613 laws, which does Jesus say is the greatest commandment? Write it out. What is the Old Testament reference for this command?

_____

_____

What is the second commandment Jesus mentions? Write it out. What is the Old Testament reference for this command?

_____

_____

_____

Interpreting the text

Why does Jesus say loving your neighbor is like loving God with all your heart, soul, and mind?

_____

_____

_____

What is Jesus saying by affirming that "all the Law and the prophets depend on these two commandments?"

_____

_____

_____

Why would God do the work of reconciliation through Christ but then entrust the message to us? What does it then mean when Paul claims to "implore [others] on behalf of Christ"?

_____

_____

_____

Teaching

Jesus says all the law and all the works of the prophets (essentially everything in the Old Testament) can be summed up in just two commands:

Love God, and love people.

Earlier in the book of Matthew, Jesus said: "Do not think I came to abolish the Law or the Prophets; I have not come to abolish them but to fulfill them," (Matthew 5:17).

So, if Jesus can sum up the Law in two sentences, and he has come to fulfill the Law, we should be asking a pretty important question: are we still bound by the Ten Commandments? What about the other 603? Is the Law still in force for us today?

In the first year of our Devoted training, we learned about the three categories of laws found in the Old Testament: **ceremonial**, **civil**, and **moral** laws. Remembering this distinction is essential to interpreting the law and loving God.[1]

Ceremonial laws covered the religious practices of the nation of Israel, including temple worship, sacrifices, and purity. These laws were perfectly fulfilled on our behalf through Jesus's sinless life and atoning death, because Jesus is both our high priest and the sacrificial lamb. The author of Hebrews reminds us of Christ's completion of the ceremonial laws:

> *But when Christ appeared as a high priest... he entered once for all into the holy places, not by means of the blood of goats and calves but by means of his own blood, thus securing an eternal redemption.*
>
> Hebrews 9:11-12

Civil laws regulated how the nation of Israel was to be governed, establishing their national identity and clarifying the responsibilities of those

---

1 Ryan Lehtinen, *Listen & Obey: Hearing God's Voice* (Clear Creek Resources, 2019), 187-190.

who were to enforce the law. These rules contain wisdom for leaders and rulers, but Jesus didn't establish his kingdom as a theocratic nation-state, as we see in his response to Pilate:

> Jesus answered, "My kingdom is not of this world. If my kingdom were of this world, my servants would have been fighting that I might not be delivered over to the Jews. But my kingdom is not from the world."
>
> John 18:36

Moral laws define what is right and wrong—good and evil—displaying God's character and values. These laws (which include the Ten Commandments) show us how our lives can reflect the holiness of God. While Jesus clearly fulfilled the moral law through a life of perfect obedience, he also upheld the moral laws of the Old Testament. Often, Jesus even intensified some moral laws (e.g. You've heard it said you shall not murder... But I say to you that everyone who is angry with his brother will be liable to judgment...). The moral laws of God are rooted in the character of God himself. Whereas religious requirements and government structures may shift over time, God's character and values are eternally unchanging.

When Jesus sums up all of the Law and Prophets with two commands, he isn't forgetting the holiness of God or the requirements put on his people to reflect that. In fact, the entire Law was originally intended to guide Israel to love God and love their neighbors. When worshippers brought their best lambs to sacrifice, they honored God by seeing it as an act of love, not duty. When the kings of Israel carried out punishments as the Law required, they loved their neighbors by reflecting God's justice. The moral law continues to show us how we can love God and love our neighbors.

Consider the first four of the Ten Commandments:
Do not have any other gods before me

Do not make anything an idol

Do not take the Lord's name in vain

Honor the Sabbath and keep it holy

These commands reflect the way we love God. They are vertical relational commands.

The final six have a different emphasis:

Honor your father and mother

Do not murder

Do not commit adultery

Do not steal

Do not bear false witness

Do not covet

Each of these laws reflect the way we love people. They are *horizontal relational commands.*

When Jesus is asked to name the greatest commandment, he answers the lawyer without hesitation. Love God. Love people. He sums up the Ten Commandments (and the other 603 laws) by saying it's all about love. So, the Law then is not burdensome and onerous. The Law has been perfectly fulfilled in Christ. We receive his perfect obedience when we trust in him for salvation. And because of that gift, we are called to respond to God's love with a love of our own: loving God and loving people as an act of wholehearted devotion.

Questions for Reflection

Outside of the Ten Commandments, what are some other moral laws that we are called to listen to and obey, because they reflect God's character? (e.g. You shall be holy, for I the Lord your God am holy —Leviticus 19:2)

_____

_____

_____

Why does it matter that Jesus fulfilled and upheld the Old Testament law rather than abolishing it? What does this show us about who God is and how he works?

_____

_____

_____

Is it possible to love God and not love people? Is it possible to truly love people and not love God? What does it look like when we try to follow one of these commands while ignoring the other?

_____

_____

_____

Prayer

Thank Jesus for fulfilling the law on your behalf. Acknowledge that his life, death, and resurrection fulfilled any obligation we might have to keep any set of laws. Repent of any legalistic patterns in your life concerning the Law, and express your love to the Father, the Son, and the Spirit for guiding us to truth in Scripture.

SCRIPTURE MEMORY

_____: The Lord our God,

the Lord is one. You shall love____

_____with all_____

and with all_____and with all

_____.

—*Deuteronomy 6:4-5*

LOVE LIVED

Scripture Study

1 CORINTHIANS 13:1-13

If I speak in the tongues of men and of angels, but have not love, I am a noisy gong or a clanging cymbal. ²And if I have prophetic powers, and understand all mysteries and all knowledge, and if I have all faith, so as to remove mountains, but have not love, I am nothing. ³If I give away all I have, and if I deliver up my body to be burned, but have not love, I gain nothing.

⁴Love is patient and kind; love does not envy or boast; it is not arrogant ⁵or rude. It does not insist on its own way; it is not irritable or resentful; ⁶it does not rejoice at wrongdoing, but rejoices with the truth. ⁷Love bears all things, believes all things, hopes all things, endures all things.

⁸Love never ends. As for prophecies, they will pass away; as for tongues, they will cease; as for knowledge, it will pass away. ⁹For we know in part and we prophesy in part, ¹⁰but when the perfect comes, the partial will pass away. ¹¹When I was a child, I spoke like a child, I thought like a child, I reasoned like a child. When I became a man, I gave up childish ways. ¹²For now we see in a mirror dimly, but then face to face. Now I know in part; then I shall know fully, even as I have been fully known.

13So now faith, hope, and love abide, these three; but the greatest of these is love.

Observing the Text

How many times is the word love mentioned in the text? What does Paul say love does? What are the positive statements made?

_____

_____

_____

What does Paul say love does not do? What are the negative statements made?

_____

_____

_____

Interpreting the Text

Paul says love never ends. Even into eternity, love lasts. Why will prophecy and tongues cease in the new Heavens and new Earth, but love never end?

_____

_____

_____

Why, in comparison with faith and hope, is love the greatest?

_____

_____

_____

Consider this text in light of the Growth Grid. If people are extremely gifted or extremely knowledgeable, but they don't love, where in the Growth Grid have they erred?

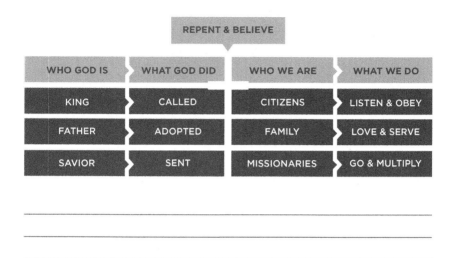

_____

_____

_____

Teaching

This week we've been talking a lot about love and how it relates to our spiritual growth. In asking how we can most clearly show our love to God, we saw that our obedience to his commands is the love language he asks us to speak. Jesus reminded us that every word of the Law can be summed up by the commands to love God and love your neighbor, because every command was designed to be followed out of wholehearted devotion.

But, how do we define love?

We might say on the same day, "I love my wife," "I love my dog," "I love the Astros," and, "I love nachos." So, is love about a relationship? Is love about a feeling? Is love about what brings me pleasure?

The Bible rarely emphasizes love as just a feeling. Most often, love is described as an action.

When we look at 1 Corinthians 13, we often have in mind a wedding ceremony. This passage is often read by a pastor before the vows, rings, and "You may kiss the bride." But notice the context in which Paul describes this kind of love. 1 Corinthians is a letter, meant to be read publicly to a church—originally, the church at Corinth. Consider the chapters surrounding this passage. In 1 Corinthians 12, Paul is talking about spiritual gifts (abilities that are empowered by the Holy Spirit and given for the purpose of serving the body). Remember, we love and serve.

That's why Paul begins chapter 13 with a warning. If you serve without love, if you are gifted or knowledgeable or have great faith, but you don't love God and love your neighbor, your service is worthless. Remember, the greatest commandment is to love God and love people.

But, what do we mean by love?

I remember hearing Joby Martin, a guest preacher for a men's event at Clear Creek, preach on 1 Corinthians 13 and go line by line through Paul's definition:

- **Love is patient and kind.** Patience is reactive. Kindness is proactive. The word for patience in the Greek has the connotation of taking a punch. It's this ability to accept the problems and sufferings that may come in relationships. There is a willingness to love despite the circumstances. Kindness is a posture we take, one of gentleness and generosity. It is especially evident when we don't stand to gain anything.
- **Love does not envy or boast.** Love isn't jealous of what other people have, nor does it brag about what it has accomplished. Our jealousy of other people (their gifts, their image, their possessions) is an affront to

God. It's an accusation that he made a mistake when he created you and provided for you.

- **Love is not arrogant or rude.** Arrogance is to think you're better than everyone else, and to be rude is to act on those thoughts.
- **Love does not insist on its own way.** The person who has to be right all the time, or make every decision, isn't usually acting out of love.
- **Love is not irritable or resentful.** Love doesn't overreact to hurt or offense. It's not easily angered and doesn't dwell on past hurts.
- **Love doesn't rejoice in wrongdoing.** Love sees sin for what it is: destructive, painful, damaging, and relationship-breaking. It responds to sin with sorrow and sincere repentance.
- **Love rejoices with the truth.** Love speaks life into people, not death. It thinks about and praises what is true, honorable, just, pure, lovely, and commendable (see Philippians 4:8).
- **Love bears all things.** This kind of love is willing to carry the weight of responsibility, of sin, of suffering, even others' sin and suffering.
- **Love believes all things.** Love chooses to believe the best about people, trusting that their intentions are good without succumbing to naiveté.
- **Love endures all things.** Love never quits. It perseveres and thrives.
- **Love never ends.** When Jesus returns and there is a new Heaven and new Earth, when we stand face to face with God in eternity, there will be no need for spiritual gifts like tongues or prophecy or teaching. We will hear from God directly. He'll reveal knowledge. We won't have a need for faith or hope in eternity. Faith is the "assurance of things hoped for, the conviction of things not seen," (Hebrews 11:1). We will see God face to face, and our faith and hope will become sight. But love lasts into eternity. That's why Paul says, "the greatest of these is love."[1]

That's a long list and long definition. We might be tempted to approach this description as just another list of things to do and not do. In fact, at the

---

1 Joby Martin, "Act Like Men." Clear Creek Community Church, Men's Event (March 2019)

men's retreat Joby challenged the guys to replace the word love in 1 Corinthians 13:4-8 with your name and ask yourself the question: How many of those statements are still true? Try it.

_____ is patient. _____ is kind. _____ does not envy or boast. _____is not irritable. _____bears all things, believes all things, endures all things.

I don't know about you, but I'm batting less than .200.

Instead, what if we replace the word love with Jesus's name? *Jesus* is patient and kind with you. *Jesus* doesn't envy (God is a jealous God, but he is jealous for you, not of you). *Jesus* doesn't boast. *Jesus* is not arrogant or rude. He doesn't insist on his own way (he submits to the Father). *Jesus* is not irritable or resentful. He does not rejoice in wrongdoing (he flips tables over instead). *Jesus* rejoices with the truth. He bears all things, believes all things, endures all things. And *Jesus* never ends (he is the Alpha and Omega, the beginning and the end). Does that stir your affections for him? Does considering how Jesus loves you cause you to love him more deeply?

If we had to prove our love by perfectly following a list of rules, we'd fail every time. But Jesus fulfilled even the law of love for you. The appropriate response to his perfect love is clear. Love him back. Love like he loves. Then pour out the same kind of love to hurting people all around you.

Questions for Reflection

Based on 1 Corinthians 13 and this study, write your own succinct definition of love.

_____

_____

_____

How does Jesus's love for you cause you to respond to him? To others?

_____

_____

_____

What old ways of "loving" do you need to repent of? How does believing the gospel change your affections and, in turn, your actions?

_____

_____

_____

Prayer

Read 1 Corinthians 13:4-8 out loud, replacing love with Jesus's name. Respond by expressing your affection for him. Commit to love God and others with your actions this week.

WEEKLY EXERCISE

TEN COMMANDMENTS | LOVING INTENT

We've spent a full week studying the Ten Commandments in light of love. Spend some time now reflecting on why God would call us not only to listen and obey, but also to love and serve. Meditate on each of the commandments. What was God's loving intent in giving the Law? And how will you love God and others differently in light of the gospel this week?

Do not have any other gods before God.

God's intent for love: _____

How will you love this week?

_____

Do not make anything an idol.

God's intent for love: _____

How will you love this week?

_____

Do not take the Lord's name in vain .

God's intent for love: _____

How will you love this week?

_____

Remember the Sabbath and keep it holy.

God's intent for love: _____

How will you love this week?

_____

Honor your father and mother.

God's intent for love: _____

How will you love this week?

_____

Do not murder.

God's intent for love: _____

How will you love this week?

_____

Do not commit adultery.

God's intent for love: _____

How will you love this week?

_____

Do not steal.

God's intent for love: _____

How will you love this week?

_____

Do not bear false witness.

God's intent for love: _____

How will you love this week?

_____

Get Ready for Group

Write your memorized Scripture.

_____

_____

_____

_____

_____

What observations and interpretations of Scripture were most meaningful to you?

_____

_____

_____

_____

_____

Summarize your key takeaway(s) for this week.

_____

_____

_____

_____

_____

What will you tell the group about the results of your exercise this week?

_____

_____

_____

_____

_____

How has this week helped you better understand and apply the Spiritual Growth Grid?

_____

_____

_____

_____

_____

REPENT & BELIEVE			
WHO GOD IS	WHAT GOD DID	WHO WE ARE	WHAT WE DO
KING	CALLED	CITIZENS	LISTEN & OBEY
FATHER	ADOPTED	FAMILY	LOVE & SERVE
SAVIOR	SENT	MISSIONARIES	GO & MULTIPLY

03

THE HUMAN HEART - IDOL FACTORIES

SCRIPTURE MEMORY

If then you have been raised with Christ, seek the things that are above, where Christ is, seated at the right hand of God. Set your minds on things that are above, not on things that are on earth.

—*Colossians 3:1-2*

IDOLATRY IN THE OLD TESTAMENT

Scripture Study

EZEKIEL 14:1-7

*Then certain of the elders of Israel came to me [Ezekiel] and sat before me.
²And the word of the Lord came to me: ³"Son of man, these men have taken
their idols into their hearts, and set the stumbling block of their iniquity
before their faces. Should I indeed let myself be consulted by them? ⁴There-
fore speak to them and say to them, Thus says the Lord God: Any one of
the house of Israel who takes his idols into his heart and sets the stumbling
block of his iniquity before his face, and yet comes to the prophet, I the
Lord will answer him as he comes with the multitude of his idols, ⁵that I may
lay hold of the hearts of the house of Israel, who are all estranged from me
through their idols.*

*⁶"Therefore say to the house of Israel, Thus says the Lord God: Repent and
turn away from your idols, and turn away your faces from all your abomi-
nations. ⁷For any one of the house of Israel, or of the strangers who sojourn
in Israel, who separates himself from me, taking his idols into his heart and
putting the stumbling block of his iniquity before his face, and yet comes*

to a prophet to consult me through him, I the Lord will answer him myself.

Observing the Text

How does God describe the idols of the elders of Israel?

_____

_____

_____

What command does God give concerning their idols?

_____

_____

_____

Interpreting the Text

The phrase "stumbling block" is used throughout Ezekiel. God's commands are characterized as being a clearly marked path, and the Hebrew concept of faith carried the meaning of stability—walking easily along that path. Therefore, to "stumble" would be parallel to a lack of faith that abandons the path of obedience to God. In light of that explanation, why is idolatry considered a stumbling block?

_____

_____

_____

Why does God respond so strongly against the idols in the hearts of the elders of Israel?

_____

_____

_____

What is God's hope for the elders of Israel?

_____

_____

_____

Teaching

John Calvin is widely credited as the most prominent theologian in the second wave of the Reformation. If Martin Luther's Ninety-Five Theses ignited the Protestant Reformation, John Calvin's _Institutes of the Christian Religion_ poured gasoline on the fire. While Martin Luther took issue with the Roman Catholic Church and exposed its corrupt practices, Calvin recognized that the institutional church was not the greatest threat to faith in Jesus. Rather, the human heart was the greatest haven for idolatry and false worship in his generation and ours.

Calvin argued that "man's nature, so to speak, is a perpetual factory of idols... man's mind, full as it is of pride and boldness, dares to imagine a god according to its own capacity" and that "the mind begets an idol, and the hand gives it birth."[1]

The heart of fallen man is an idol factory.

I don't know what you imagine when you hear the word "idol," but I tend to think of a sculpture in a faraway land, an ornate temple to a false god, or some primitive form of worship. But Calvin argued, as Ezekiel did, that idols originate in man's heart. We create them.

_____

1 John Calvin, _Calvin: Institutes of the Christian Religion_ (Westminster John Knox Press, June 1960), 108

The hope for this week's study is to identify the idols of *your own* heart. If we desire to love God with wholehearted devotion, then we must begin by identifying the idols our hearts are worshiping, the idols our minds are imagining and the idols our hands are creating.

Today, let's begin with an overview of the Old Testament's teaching on idolatry.[2]

In Genesis, God created humanity with the capacity and purpose of worshiping its creator. Part of that worship included a command to rule over creation in service to God. Instead, humanity rejected God's design in favor of a prideful, selfish desire to "be like God" (Genesis 3:4). When Paul described the fall of man in Romans, he did so by illustrating their idolatry.

> *[They] exchanged the glory of the immortal God... and worshiped and served the created things rather than the Creator.*
>
> Romans 1:23-25 (NIV)

Adam and Eve, our representatives, reversed the intended order. Humanity began to worship and serve created things and were therefore ruled by them. This wasn't God's intention. It was a result of idolatry.

In our study of the Ten Commandments, we've noted the first two commands specifically address idolatry. The first prohibits worshiping other gods. The second forbids worshiping God idolatrously, forming his identity according to our desires. The following chapters warn Israel against worshiping foreign "gods," because they will ensnare you (Exodus 23:33). Moses argues that each of us will either worship God or worship some created thing (an idol); there is no third option. We are designed

---

2 Tim Keller, *Gospel In Life Study Guide: Grace Changes Everything* (Zondervan, March 2010), 37-38.

to be worshipers. Every human heart is inclined to worship, to hold allegiance to something or someone.

In the Psalms, we see the contrast between holiness and idolatry.

> *Who shall ascend the hill of the Lord?*
> *And who shall stand in his holy place?*
> *He who has clean hands and a pure heart,*
> *who does not lift up his soul to what is false...*

Psalm 24:3-4

The prophets argued that idols are empty, futile, and powerless—the work of human hands. Idols bring about spiritual blindness (Isaiah 44:18), enslave their worshippers (Jeremiah 16:13), poison the heart to complete dependence on them (Isaiah 44:17), and capture our hearts (Ezekiel 14:2).

In essence, the Old Testament teaches that idols are anything that take the rightful place of the one true God, Yahweh. Author Richard Keyes explains it this way:

> A careful reading of the Old and New Testaments shows that idolatry is nothing like the crude, simplistic picture that springs to mind of an idol sculpture in some distant country. As the main category to describe unbelief, the idea is highly sophisticated, drawing together the complexities of motivation in individual psychology, the social environment, and also the unseen world. Idols are not just on pagan altars, but in well-educated human hearts and minds... The Bible does not allow us to marginalize idolatry to the fringes of life... it is found on center stage.[3]

---

3 Richard Keyes, "The Idol Factory" in *No God but God: Breaking with the Idols of Our Age*, ed. Os Guinness and John Seel (Moody Press, September 1992), 31.

If the human heart is a factory for idols, then Keyes is right in stating that idolatry isn't a sideline issue for us; it is a center-stage concern. If we are to love the Lord with all of our heart—if full devotion to God has always been his plan—then we must do the hard work of identifying the idols our hearts are producing.

Questions for Reflection

What did John Calvin mean by describing the human heart as a factory of idols? How do our minds and hands contribute to this?

_____

_____

_____

What is the consistent teaching on idolatry throughout the Old Testament? Why should this matter to us today?

_____

_____

_____

Every human heart is inclined to worship something or someone. Outside of faithfully worshiping God, what idols do you think your heart is creating, desiring, and intending to worship?

_____

_____

_____

Prayer

Ask God to reveal the idols your heart is creating and give you a desire to worship only Him. Pray that he would renew your mind and give your hands faithful work to participate in this week.

SCRIPTURE MEMORY

If then you have been raised with
Christ,_____the things that are
above, where Christ is, seated at the
right hand of God. Set your_____
on things that are above, not on
things that are on_____.

—*Colossians 3:1-2*

IDOLATRY IN THE NEW TESTAMENT

Scripture Study

ROMANS 1:18-25

For the wrath of God is revealed from heaven against all ungodliness and unrighteousness of men, who by their unrighteousness suppress the truth. [19]For what can be known about God is plain to them, because God has shown it to them. [20]For his invisible attributes, namely, his eternal power and divine nature, have been clearly perceived, ever since the creation of the world, in the things that have been made. So, they are without excuse. [21]For although they knew God, they did not honor him as God or give thanks to him, but they became futile in their thinking, and their foolish hearts were darkened. [22]Claiming to be wise, they became fools, [23]and exchanged the glory of the immortal God for images resembling mortal man and birds and animals and creeping things.

[24]Therefore God gave them up in the lusts of their hearts to impurity, to the dishonoring of their bodies among themselves, [25]because they exchanged the truth about God for a lie and worshiped and served the creature rather than the Creator, who is blessed forever! Amen.

Observing the text

What can be known about God's character by simply observing his creation (verses 19-20)?

_____

_____

List the character traits of humanity described in this passage.

_____

_____

_____

Describe in your own words the "exchange" depicted in verses 22-25.

_____

_____

_____

Interpreting the text

According to this passage, what reasons are behind the human propensity to create and worship idols?

_____

_____

_____

What are some present-day examples of people worshiping created things rather than the Creator?

_____

_____

_____

Teaching

What are you willing to do and what are you willing to give up to be the best you can be? You only have so much energy and the clock ticks on all of us… If you're going to compete against me, you better be willing to give your life, because I'm giving up mine.[1]

Tom Brady, Quarterback, New England Patriots

Tom Brady is an anomaly. In 2018, when the average age of an NFL starting quarterback was 29 years old, Tom Brady won the Super Bowl at age 41. He attributes his success to a number of factors, including a radically disciplined diet and workout regimen, but primarily to his overwhelming will to win. Nothing matters more to Tom Brady than winning football games. Even Gisele Bündchen, Brady's supermodel wife, said his first love is football. It's an inordinate desire.

The Greek word *epithumiai* can be translated "desire, passionate longing, lust, and inordinate desire." If the Old Testament used the concept of idolatry to characterize our drift from God, then the New Testament equivalent is the idea of desires *(epithumiai)*. The New Testament merges the concept of idolatry with these excessive, life-ruling desires of the heart.[2] Notice, idolatry stems from the heart and likewise, inordinate desires.

Remember, the human heart is an idol factory.

---

1 *Tom vs. Time.* Episode 1 "The Physical Game," Directed by Gotham Chopra, aired January 25, 2018, on Facebook Watch, https://www.facebook.com/vsonwatch/videos/2081108082122933/.
2 Tim Keller, *Gospel In Life Study Guide: Grace Changes Everything* (Zondervan, March 2010), 37-38.

Let's look at some key New Testament texts that point us toward the heart issue of idolatry and inordinate desires.

Romans 1:18-25, the passage we studied today, reveals that we create idols because we desire to control our own lives. Despite our knowledge of God, at times we choose not to glorify or thank him because we want to be in control. We, instead, set our hearts on created things rather than on God, and in turn, build our lives and desires around them. These inordinate desires are the idols of our hearts. We are compelled to worship something, so we create substitute gods. We "exchange the truth of God for a lie" (Romans 1:25).

In his letter to the church in Galatia, Paul describes this exchange as slavery.

> *Formerly, when you did not know God, you were enslaved to those that by nature are not gods. But now that you have come to know God, or rather to be known by God, how can you turn back again to the weak and worthless elementary principles of the world, whose slaves you want to be once more?*
>
> Galatians 4:8-9

Paul warns the Galatians, these gospel-believers, not to slide back into a form of idolatry, where the values of the world outweigh their desires for a holy creator God. This admonition came when a group of religious zealots were insisting that the Galatian Christians be circumcised in order to secure their salvation—essentially a form of moralistic legalism. Paul likens this to returning to idolatry. The implications of his warning are significant. If you believe that anything other than Christ is necessary for salvation, that's idolatry. Something other than God has become your ultimate hope, and that inordinate desire will ultimately enslave you.

The book of 1 John is a letter to the church concerning assurance of salvation. John has written five chapters about living in the light, loving your neighbor, and obedience to God. Then, in the last verse, John writes this: "Little children, keep yourselves from idols" (5:21). Idolatry hasn't been mentioned once in the letter up to this point. Tim Keller argues that either John is now, in the last sentence, changing the subject completely, or he is summarizing the entire letter with this one caution. The latter seems more likely. In the last sentence, John reiterates his argument that to walk in holiness, love, and truth is to keep yourselves from idols. Any failure to walk according to God's way is another form of idolatry.[3]

So why do we lie, become greedy, seek power, or lust after personal fulfillment? Why would we give our entire lives to winning? Each of these choices is fueled by the belief that there is something other than God that we need in order to be fulfilled.

We have inordinate desires. Translation: our hearts are idol factories.

Questions for Reflection

What is one thing you'd be willing to give your whole life for?

_____

_____

_____

How would you define inordinate desire in your own words?

_____

_____

_____

---

3 Ibid. 40.

Have you ever felt enslaved by an inordinate desire? Describe your experience.

_____

_____

_____

Prayer

Confess the inordinate desires of your heart to God. Acknowledge the ways you have taken created things and made them ultimate things. Ask God to continue to reveal areas of your heart that are not yet pure and wholly his.

SCRIPTURE MEMORY

If then you have been_____with

_____, seek the things that are

_____, where Christ is, seated at the

right hand of God. Set your minds

on things that are_____, not on

things that are on earth.

—Colossians 3:1-2

IDENTIFYING YOUR IDOLS

Scripture Study

GALATIANS 4:8-9

Formerly, when you did not know God, you were enslaved to those that by nature are not gods. ⁹But now that you have come to know God, or rather to be known by God, how can you turn back again to the weak and worthless elementary principles of the world, whose slaves you want to be once more?

Observing the Text

Is Paul writing to believers or non-believers in this passage?

_____

_____

_____

List the two synonymous phrases that Paul uses to describe idols.

_____

_____

_____

What is the result of turning back to idols?

_____

_____

_____

Interpreting the Text

Why does Paul compare idolatry to slavery?

_____

_____

_____

If "repentance" means turning to God, then why are the Galatians now returning to an old way of living? How often do you find yourself returning to an old way of living?

_____

_____

_____

Teaching

If wholehearted devotion to God was always his plan, and he commands us to love him with all of our heart, then we have a problem.

As Calvin said, our hearts are idol factories. God's desire for us is a thrilling love relationship with him, and perfect community with the Father, the Son, and the Holy Spirit. Unfortunately, sin in our lives causes us to consider alternative relationships and alternative desires. We've exchanged the truth of God for a lie. We'd rather worship the creation than the creator.

Thus, in order to really love God with all of our hearts, we must identify the idols our hearts are creating. But, in a world full of potential idols, how do we know when something has become an idol? Richard Keyes in his essay "The Idol Factory" writes:

> As soon as our loyalty to anything leads us to disobey God, we are in danger of making it an idol... An idol can be a physical object, a property, a person, an activity, a role, an institution, a hope, an image, an idea, a pleasure, a hero.[1]

Today is less of an exercise in teaching and more in training – the hard work of unearthing the inordinate desires of your specific heart.

Let's use this definition to guide our work today:

> An idol is anything more important to you than God, anything that absorbs your heart and imagination more than God, and anything you seek to give you what only God can give.[2]

Questions for Reflection

What are your greatest fears? What do you worry most about?

_____

_____

_____

What do you rely on for comfort after a long day? When life is hard, what/who do you turn to first?

_____

_____

_____

---

1 Richard Keyes, "The Idol Factory" in *No God but God: Breaking with the Idols of Our Age*, ed. Os Guinness and John Seel (Moody Press, September 1992), 31.
2 Tim Keller, *Counterfeit Gods*, (Dutton, October 2009), xix.

What gives you the greatest sense of self-worth? What are you proudest of?

_____

_____

_____

What is one thing that if you didn't have it, would make life less worth living?

_____

_____

_____

What do you really want and expect out of life? What would really make you happy?

_____

_____

_____

Read through the following statements[3] and check any/all of those that most resonate with you:

☐ Life only has meaning/I only have worth if... I have power and influence over others. (Power Idolatry)

☐ Life only has meaning/I only have worth if...I am loved and respected by _____. (Approval Idolatry)
Life only has meaning/I only have worth if... I have this kind of pleasure experience, a particular quality of life. (Comfort Idolatry)

☐ Life only has meaning/I only have worth if... I am able to get mastery

---

3 Tim Keller, *Gospel In Life Study Guide: Grace Changes Everything* (Zondervan, March 2010), 43.

over my life in the area of _____. (Comfort Idolatry)

☐ Life only has meaning/I only have worth if... people are dependent on me and need me. (Helping Idolatry)

☐ Life only has meaning/I only have worth if... someone is there to protect me and keep me safe. (Dependence Idolatry)

☐ Life only has meaning/I only have worth if... I am completely free from obligations or responsibilities to take care of someone. (Independence Idolatry)

☐ Life only has meaning/I only have worth if... I am highly productive and get a lot done. (Work Idolatry)

☐ Life only has meaning/I only have worth if... I am being recognized for my accomplishments and excelling in my work. (Achievement Idolatry)

☐ Life only has meaning/ I only have worth if... I have a certain level of wealth, financial freedom, and very nice possessions. (Materialism Idolatry)

☐ Life only has meaning/I only have worth if... I am adhering to my religion's moral codes and accomplished in its activities. (Religion Idolatry)

☐ Life only has meaning/I only have worth if... this one person is in my life and is happy to be there, and /or happy with me. (Individual Person Idolatry)

☐ Life only has meaning/I only have worth if... I feel totally independent of organized religion and am living by a self-made morality. (Irreligion Idolatry)

☐ Life only has meaning/I only have worth if... my race and culture is ascendant and recognized as superior. (Racial/Cultural Idolatry)

☐ Life only has meaning/ I only have worth if... a particular social grouping or professional grouping or other group lets me in. (Inner-ring Idolatry)

☐ Life only has meaning/I only have worth if... my children and/or my parents are happy and happy with me. (Family Idolatry)

☐ Life only has meaning/I only have worth if... Mr. or Ms. Right is in love with me. (Relationship Idolatry)

☐ Life only has meaning/only have worth if... I am hurting, in a problem, only then do I feel worthy of love or able to deal with guilt. (Suffering Idolatry)

☐ Life only has meaning/ I only have worth if... my political or social cause is making progress and ascending in influence or power. (Ideology Idolatry)

☐ Life only has meaning/ I only have worth if... I have a particular kind of look or body image. (Image Idolatry)

Prayer

Be honest with God about the state of your heart, where you see certain idols surfacing. Confess sin. Then, spend two minutes in silence, allowing God to encourage you with his presence and remind you of your identity in Christ.

WEEKLY EXERCISE

IDENTIFYING IDOLS AND THEIR EFFECTS

Refer back to the statements on pages 92-94.

Look for common themes. What things tend to be too important to you?

_____

_____

_____

What are your idols?

_____

_____

_____

The first four statements are pretty common, over-arching idolatries for many of us. Fill in the blanks in the chart below identifying the effects of these specific idols and then answer the questions below.

If you seek POWER (success, winning, influence)	If you seek AFFIRMATION (affirmation, love, relationships)
Your greatest nightmare: *Humiliation*	Your greatest nightmare: *Rejection*
People around you often feel: *Used*	People around you often feel: *Smothered*
Your problem emotion: *Anger*	Your problem emotion: *Cowardice*
Your identity is often found in...	**Your identity is often found in...**
_____	_____
In order to repent of this idol, one must...	**In order to repent of this idol, one must...**
_____	_____

If you seek COMFORT (privacy, lack of stress, freedom)	If you seek CONTROL (self-discipline, certainty, standards)
Your greatest nightmare: *Stress, demands*	Your greatest nightmare: *Uncertainty*
People around you often feel: *Neglected*	People around you often feel: *Condemned*
Your problem emotion: *Boredom*	Your problem emotion: *Worry*
Your identity is often found in...	**Your identity is often found in...**
_____	_____
In order to repent of this idol, one must...	**In order to repent of this idol, one must...**
_____	_____

Get feedback from others about this evaluation. Ask your spouse and/or a few close friends if they agree with the idols you identified and whether they have felt the effects of those idols in your relationship/friendship. What do they notice about your priorities, values, and motives that you might not be seeing?

_____

_____

_____

Get Ready for Group

Write your memorized Scripture.

_____

_____

_____

_____

_____

What observations and interpretations of Scripture were most meaningful to you?

_____

_____

_____

_____

_____

Summarize your key takeaway(s) for this week.

_____

_____

_____

_____

_____

What will you tell the group about the results of your exercise this week?

_____

_____

_____

_____

How has this week helped you better understand and apply the Spiritual Growth Grid?

_____

_____

_____

_____

_____

REPENT & BELIEVE			
WHO GOD IS	**WHAT GOD DID**	**WHO WE ARE**	**WHAT WE DO**
KING	CALLED	CITIZENS	LISTEN & OBEY
FATHER	ADOPTED	FAMILY	LOVE & SERVE
SAVIOR	SENT	MISSIONARIES	GO & MULTIPLY

04

HEART SURGERY - DISPLACING IDOLS

SCRIPTURE MEMORY

If then you have been raised with Christ, seek the things that are above, where Christ is, seated at the right hand of God. Set your minds on things that are above, not on things that are on earth.

—*Colossians 3:1-2*

DISPLACING YOUR IDOLS

Scripture Study

COLOSSIANS 3:1-4

If then you have been raised with Christ, seek the things that are above, where Christ is, seated at the right hand of God. ²Set your minds on things that are above, not on things that are on earth. ³For you have died, and your life is hidden with Christ in God. ⁴When Christ who is your life appears, then you also will appear with him in glory.

Observing the Text

What are the primary commands in this passage?

_____

_____

_____

List any identity statements Paul makes about his readers

_____

_____

_____

How does Paul use the imagery of life and death to describe our relationship with Christ?

_____

_____

_____

Interpreting the Text

In verse 1, why is Paul's command contingent upon the reader "being raised with Christ"?

_____

_____

_____

If "your life is hidden with Christ in God", how does that impact your identity in comparison with his?

_____

_____

_____

Consider the Spiritual Growth Grid

In what ways does your life/identity reflect the identity of God? In what ways are you struggling to reflect Christ this week?

_____

_____

_____

Teaching

Change or die. Can you imagine being given that choice?

Let's say you've been experiencing some chest pain. Your doctor runs some tests and discovers that you have a life-or-death decision to make: either continue to live the way you have been with an extraordinary risk of a heart attack, or opt for surgery. This surgery will bypass a blocked artery and allow your heart to function at maximum capacity. But after the surgery, your diet must change, your exercise rhythms must change, your stress-levels must be reduced. Would you be willing to make the change?

According to a recent study, about 600,000 bypass surgeries are performed each year, and another 1.3 million angioplasties. These procedures will temporarily relieve chest pains, but the patients must also make significant lifestyle changes in order to sustain their cardiac health. Dr. Edward Miller, dean of the medical school at John Hopkins University, stated, "If you look at people after coronary-artery bypass grafting, two years later, ninety percent of them have not changed their lifestyle... Even though they know they have a very bad disease and they know they should change, for whatever reason, they can't." [1]

---

1 Alan Deutschman, "Change or Die," _Fast Company_ (May 2005), https://www.fastcompany.com/52717/change-or-die.

Last week, we identified the human heart as a factory for idols. God intended for us to love him with all our hearts, and yet because of sin, we produce substitute gods – idols – instead. Our hearts worship created things rather than the Creator himself. We have two options: continue to live the way we have, or do the hard work of displacing the idols that have a grip on our heart. It's one thing to identify idols, it's another thing entirely to root them out.

We must change or die.

So how does one go about displacing idols? Today, we will focus on three approaches to personal change and then challenge each other to take hold of lasting spiritual health.

The **"moralizing" approach** focuses on behavior:[2]

> Your problem is that you are doing wrong and have sin in your life, so repent! Change your actions so that they are in line with the rules.

But, focusing on behavior alone is insufficient. We must understand the why behind the what in order to address the real heart issue. As we've seen in the spiritual growth grid, our activity is often driven by our identity. By focusing on behavior alone, we may patch up some surface-level issues, but in order to really transform the heart we must address the sin beneath the sin.

Why do I desire something other than God? What inordinate desires are in my heart? What idols have taken root in my life? Repenting of behavior alone will always prove inadequate, because there is an underlying belief

---

22 Tim Keller, *Gospel In Life Study Guide: Grace Changes Everything* (Zondervan, March 2010), 45.

that if I don't have this thing or this person or this image, then I am still a failure. We must go deeper than behavior.

The **"psychologizing" approach** focuses on feelings, which seem to be deeper than behavior:[3]

> Your problem is that you don't see that God loves you as you are, so believe! Believe that you are created in his image, and that you have worth. Feel loved by God.

But, focusing on feelings still fails to plumb the depths needed to see real change. We must also ask why we feel the way we do. Why do I feel despair (or anger, or fear) when circumstances threaten my priorities and treasures? What inordinate desires are causing this? What are the idols behind these false beliefs?

Telling someone to "repent and change" is insufficient because it only addresses behavior. Telling someone to "feel loved by God" is still insufficient because it only addresses a feeling.

But, the third approach to displacing idols not only addresses the sin underlying our particular behaviors but addresses our feelings as well.

This third way is simply **the Gospel**:

> Your problem is that you are looking to something besides Christ for your happiness; you've been worshiping an idol and rejecting the one true God. Repent and believe in the Gospel!

The real sin beneath the sin isn't a behavior or a feeling. In our heart of hearts, we are trusting in something other than Christ for our happiness,

---

3 Ibid, pg. 45

our worth and our salvation. Every idol we have identified in the previous week is a way of salvation by works:

- I only have worth if I have power and influence.
- Life only has meaning if I am loved and respected by others
- I will only experience joy if I have this particular quality of life.
- I am only worthy if I am in control.

Each of these statements are not only idolatrous but also enslaving. When we find our worth in anything other than who God says we are in Christ, we assume that salvation requires God's grace plus our works. Grace plus power. Grace plus control.

The Apostle Paul tells us in Romans 6:14, "Sin shall not be your master, because you are not under law, but under grace."

We will only be "under grace," and experience freedom from idols, when we repent of the idols in our hearts and rest and rejoice in the saving work and love of Christ.

To really displace idols, we must replace them with the particular things Jesus provides through the gospel. When we struggle with power or control, we must repent of a success-driven mentality and believe that God is King, who has called us to be citizens. When we struggle with self-worth or approval, we must repent of seeking affirmation, and believe that God is a Father who has adopted us as his children. When we struggle with a desire for comfort and ease, we must repent and believe that God is a Savior who has sent us to be missionaries.

Idols clog up our hearts. They rob us of the fullness of joy God intended. We need drastic measures—heart surgeries—to bypass old ways of living and replace them with new affections. Christ has done the work at the cross. Now, he calls us to repent and believe in the gospel. This is the only way we change.

Questions for Reflection

Why does behavior modification rarely result in real life change?

_____

_____

_____

Why is belief alone inadequate for displacing an idol?

_____

_____

_____

How does repenting and believing in the gospel address your specific idols that we identified last week?

_____

_____

_____

Prayer

Confess to God the things you have built your life around. Confess that these things may be good things that you have made ultimate things. Praise God for being the source of everything you need. Give God space and time to remind you of the gospel's work in your life to displace old ways of living.

SCRIPTURE MEMORY

If then you have been raised with Christ,_____that are above,_____, seated at the right hand of God. Set your minds on things that are above, not on things that are on earth.

—*Colossians 3:1-2*

MORTIFICATION

Scripture Study

COLOSSIANS 3:5-11

Put to death therefore what is earthly in you: sexual immorality, impurity, passion, evil desire, and covetousness, which is idolatry. ⁶On account of these the wrath of God is coming. ⁷In these you too once walked, when you were living in them. ⁸But now you must put them all away: anger, wrath, malice, slander, and obscene talk from your mouth. ⁹Do not lie to one another, seeing that you have put off the old self with its practices ¹⁰and have put on the new self, which is being renewed in knowledge after the image of its creator. ¹¹Here there is not Greek and Jew, circumcised and uncircumcised, barbarian, Scythian, slave, free; but Christ is all, and in all..

Observing the text

List all of the activities and attitudes that Paul commands believers to put to death or put away.

_____

_____

_____

How does Paul describe the new self that we have put on?

_____

_____

_____

What identity statements are made about the readers?

_____

_____

_____

Interpreting the text

In verse 5, when Paul says, "which is idolatry" do you think he is referring solely to covetousness, or is this in reference to the entire list of sins he has just described? In what ways is idolatry at the root of each of them?

_____

_____

_____

What changes does the gospel make concerning God's wrath, concerning sin, and concerning our identity?

_____

_____

_____

Teaching

John Owen, the great Puritan preacher, once famously wrote, "Be killing sin, or it will be killing you."[1] Owen is echoing Colossian 3:5, "Put to death, therefore, whatever is earthly in you..." We are only able to seek the things

---

1 John Owen, *On the Mortification of Sin in Believers* (Banner of Truth, May 2004), 9.

that are above and love the Lord with all of our hearts when we begin by putting to death old ways of living and our old identities.

Owen didn't just give us a quotable phrase on killing sin. He wrote a whole treatise on the subject entitled *On the Mortification of Sin in Believers*, originally intended to help Puritan teenagers in their fight against immorality. Owen argues that success in ridding our hearts of idols starts with the recognition that we are engaged in a battle.

Mortification, in a theological context, is not akin to a feeling of shame or embarrassment as we tend to use the word mortified. Rather, it means to kill or subdue—to murder the inordinate desires resident within us. Paul lists some examples in Colossians 3: sexual immorality, impurity, passion, evil desire, and covetousness, which is equated with idolatry. Paul literally says to mortify them, to murder these old ways of living.

So why must we mortify sin? Why must we do the hard work of heart surgery on our personal idols? John Owen gives three arguments for the necessity of killing sin:

Sin is always active.
Because we still live in a broken world, God has not yet freed us from the presence of sin in our lives. The attack of temptation won't stop until we leave this world.

Unaddressed sin weakens and darkens our souls.
When sin is left stagnant in our lives and hearts, we quickly become accustomed to its presence there. Its continual company leaves us doubting God's work to transform us, stealing both our hope and joy.

Unaddressed sin in our lives hardens others around us to the beauty of the gospel.

An unwillingness to fight our own sin harms not only ourselves, but anyone who is observing our choices and actions. When we testify that God's ways are good but refuse to walk in them, the goodness of Christ's work to cleanse us is hidden from sight.

To mortify sin does not mean we will utterly destroy it. That's the Holy Spirit's work in us, not something we are capable of on our own. Rather, mortification is a habitual weakening of sin in our lives, a constant fight against it, and freedom from its control.

So how do we do that? How do we mortify sin?

1. **We repent and believe in the gospel.** It's what we argued for in Day 1— we preach the gospel to ourselves by filling our souls with the consideration of who Jesus is and what he has done for us.

2. **We rely on the Holy Spirit.** "A man may easier see without eyes and speak without a tongue, than mortify a sin without the Spirit." We must pray for God to do in us what we cannot do on our own.

3. **We must intend to obey God in every area of our lives.** When faced with temptation, if we love our sin more than we love Jesus, we will obey our idols, rather than listen to and obey the voice of God.

4. **We must hate sin.** "Christ is never loved 'til sin be loathed."[2]

One of the ways we cultivate a hatred for sin is to reflect on the great cost of it—not only in terms of its worldly consequences (strife, war, envy, greed, lust, conflict, etc.), but also acknowledging that our sin ultimately led to the crucifixion of Jesus on our behalf. Reflecting on that truth should galvanize our hatred for sin. And when a Christian hates their sin, they will seek to rid themselves of all of it, not just some of it. We don't just repent of a particular sin while secretly harboring others, but submit ourselves to God's will in every area of our lives.[3]

---

2 Thomas Watson, *The Doctrine of Repentance* (Banner of Truth, January 1988), 40.
3 Yancey Arrington, *Tap: Defeating the Sins that Defeat You* (Clear Creek Resources, July

So, is mortification our work or God's? Is repentance something I do or something God does in me? The answer to both questions is "yes." This is the mystery of the gospel. It is a work of God's grace in us *and* something in which we take part. It is both a grace given, and an effort exercised. So, we pray, asking God for the strength to repent, and then we run headlong into killing sin, lest we be killed by it.

The mortification of sin isn't intended to be a killjoy. Instead, God intends that by killing sin we might experience a far greater joy.

Questions for Reflection

What does it look like when unaddressed sin weakens and darkens our souls?

_____

_____

_____

To what degree do you hate your sin? What evidences in your life point to this reality?

_____

_____

_____

Describe God's work in mortification and our own. What next step is God calling you to take when it comes to killing personal sin and discarding your idols?

_____

_____

_____

2010), 86-94

Prayer

Ask God for the strength to repent of habitual sin. Rely on the Holy Spirit to reveal any sin you haven't yet addressed. Confess your hatred for it, and commit this week to take a step to kill sin in your life.

SCRIPTURE MEMORY

If then you have been raised with Christ, seek the things that are above, where Christ is,_____ _____God. Set your minds on_____, not on things that are on earth.

—Colossians 3:1-2

VIVIFICATION

Scripture Study

COLOSSIANS 3:11-17

Here there is not Greek and Jew, circumcised and uncircumcised, barbarian, Scythian, slave, free; but Christ is all, and in all. ¹²Put on then, as God's chosen ones, holy and beloved, compassionate hearts, kindness, humility, meekness, and patience, ¹³bearing with one another and, if one has a complaint against another, forgiving each other; as the Lord has forgiven you, so you also must forgive. ¹⁴And above all these put on love, which binds everything together in perfect harmony. ¹⁵And let the peace of Christ rule in your hearts, to which indeed you were called in one body. And be thankful. ¹⁶Let the word of Christ dwell in you richly, teaching and admonishing one another in all wisdom, singing psalms and hymns and spiritual songs, with thankfulness in your hearts to God. ¹⁷And whatever you do, in word or deed, do everything in the name of the Lord Jesus, giving thanks to God the Father through him.

Observing the Text

List the things Paul commands we "put on."

_____

_____

_____

What is the "word of Christ" intended to do in the heart of the believer?

_____

_____

Underline any reference to "thankfulness" in the passage. Define thankfulness below.

_____

_____

_____

Interpreting the Text

Notice how many of the things we are commanded to put on in verses 12-17 require a community of people to practice them with. Why is Christian community essential in following Jesus the way Scripture commands?

_____

_____

_____

Verse 11, and the beginning of verse 12, gives context to the commands listed afterwards. Why is it important to recognize our gospel identity before we consider gospel activity (things we are commanded to "put on")?

_____

_____

_____

Why does Paul focus so much on thankfulness as he concludes this section of his letter to the Colossians? Is that attitude in contrast to how you might naturally approach the commands of God?

_____

_____

_____

Teaching

If mortification is to kill or subdue – to murder inordinate desires resident in us—then vivification is the positive side of the coin. It implies adding life, quality, or energy to something. If mortification is playing defense, vivification is going on offense.

In Colossians 3, not only does Paul say to "put to death" (mortify) certain ways of living, but he insists that those who find their identity in Christ will "put on" (vivify) a new way of living. The work of the Holy Spirit to progressively sanctify the believer is worked out in both mortification and vivification. Both are primarily a work of the Holy Spirit, and yet, we play a roll in putting to death inordinate desires and breathing life into godly desires.

One of my East Texas pastor friends used to say it this way: "Don't just pull weeds—plant grass."

Often, unruly weeds get a foothold in our yards because there are areas of the lawn where the grass is too thin or weak. Weeds take advantage of any space where grass is not thriving and then threatens to take over the whole yard. Landscapers know the key to a healthy lawn isn't just the removal of weeds but stronger grass. Along the Gulf Coast, St. Augustine grass grows well in most areas. By nature, St. Augustine is one of the more aggressive and competitive strain of grass. It takes over areas. It chokes out weeds. In fact, if allowed, St. Augustine could overtake and kill most shrubs in your yard.

So, twice a year I do what most of you do—I "weed and feed" my yard. I apply a fertilizer that is specially designed to kill the weeds and feed the desired grass. If I only focused on killing weeds, they'd eventually grow back. But, if I feed the healthy grass in my yard, the St. Augustine will eventually take over, grow a lush lawn, and all the weeds will be gone.

Spiritually speaking, we need a weed-and-feed strategy. When displacing idols in our lives or fighting sin, we often focus on killing the weeds. We concentrate on the mortification of sin and ridding ourselves of old ways of living. But what if the best way to rid our hearts of idols wasn't just a good weed killer but also a focus on helping the grass grow with healthy spiritual rhythms? In sports, we might say it this way: the best defense is a really good offense.

Take for example a man's struggle with pornography, knowing that the root of that sin could be any number of idols (power, control, comfort, relationships, etc.). In order to rid his heart of a specific idol, he might focus on some defensive measures: fleeing sexual immorality, having accountability, praying God removes the temptation, getting to the root of the desire. These are great defensive strategies. They are focused on pulling weeds. But, on its own, a singular focus on not doing something can have negative results. If you tell yourself over and over again not to do something, the desire to do so could actually increase. Therefore, he must replace that time and energy with a focus on some healthy rhythms. He must fertilize the grass of his heart by pursuing a robust love for Jesus, cultivating healthy rhythms of Scripture reading and memorization, pursuing appropriate intimacy in a marriage relationship, or having a healthy view of the opposite sex. These are offensive measures.

Or take a woman's struggle with greed, again acknowledging that the root of that sin is a deeper idol (materialism, comfort, image, etc.). She may pull weeds by confessing her sin to her small group, removing tempting situations, or going on a spending fast. But equally important, she must grow her heart for the Lord: acknowledge he is the owner of everything, practice generosity in all resources (time, money, and energy). By saying "yes" to God, she is simultaneously saying "no" to sin—mortification and vivification.

Remember, God's desire is not just to rid us of old ways of living and harmful behaviors, but for the gospel to take such root in our hearts that it would breathe life, energy, joy, and love into us. Our hope isn't only that our hearts would cease to produce idols. God's command is to love him with all of our hearts, but that is only possible when we fertilize the grass, when we grow our desire for him. Scottish pastor Thomas Chalmers talked of this expulsive power of a new affection, arguing that "misplaced affections need to be replaced by the far greater power of the affection of the Gospel."[1] So, pull weeds! Do the hard work of displacing idols. But also, plant grass. Do so in a way that grows an abiding affection for God, that generates the kind of life-giving love, joy, peace, patience, kindness, goodness, faithfulness, gentleness, and self-control that Scripture describes (Galatians 5:22).

When it comes to displacing idols, mortification and vivification are two of the ways the Holy Spirit causes us to grow our affections for God. But, lest we despair when we fail, or get arrogant when we succeed, be reminded that it is God who causes the grass to grow and God who sanctifies his saints. We "put to death" the things of the flesh and "put on" the works of the Spirit, but we acknowledge that God is the one truly at work in both.

Questions for Reflection

Which is easier for you to focus on, mortification or vivification? Why?

_____

_____

_____

---

1 Thomas Chalmers, *The Expulsive Power of a New Affection*, (Reprinted by Curiosmith, May 2012).

What will happen if we choose one to the neglect of the other? How have you seen that happen in your own life?

_____

_____

_____

Today's teaching gave two examples of applying both mortification and vivification to sin issues. Identify a personal sin struggle and its root idol, then give examples of how you might apply mortification and vivification principles in your life to displace that idol.

_____

_____

_____

_____

_____

_____

_____

Prayer

Pray through the last question in today's reflection, confessing your sin to God. Ask him to reveal the sin beneath the sin – the idolatry of your heart. Allow God to guide your steps of mortification and give clarity on how to vivify (enliven or energize) your pursuit of displacing idols. Enjoy time in God's presence, knowing it is an act of God's grace to make you look more and more like his son Jesus.

WEEKLY EXERCISE

WORSHIP THROUGH PSALM 115

The Psalms were written as lyrical poetry and often sung in corporate worship, encouraging the reader to praise God for who he is and what he has done. The Psalms are intended to grow our love for God, not just stimulate our minds. Today, read Psalm 115 in an act of worship. Allow it to stir your affections for God, then write your own version of this Psalm with what you have learned this week through God revealing your idols. The aim of this week's exercise is worship—to love the Lord your God with all your heart.

> [1] *Not to us, O Lord, not to us, but to your name give glory,*
>   *for the sake of your steadfast love and your faithfulness!*
> [2] *Why should the nations say, "Where is their God?"*
> [3] *Our God is in the heavens; he does all that he pleases.*
>
> [4] *Their idols are silver and gold, the work of human hands.*
> [5] *They have mouths, but do not speak; eyes, but do not see.*
> [6] *They have ears, but do not hear; noses, but do not smell.*
> [7] *They have hands, but do not feel; feet, but do not walk;*
>   *and they do not make a sound in their throat.*
> [8] *Those who make them become like them; so do all who trust in them.*
>
> [9] *O Israel, trust in the Lord! He is their help and their shield.*
> [10] *O house of Aaron, trust in the Lord! He is their help and their shield.*
> [11] *You who fear the Lord, trust in the Lord! He is their help and their shield.*
> [12] *The Lord has remembered us; he will bless us; he will bless the house of Israel;*

he will bless the house of Aaron;

[13] he will bless those who fear the Lord, both the small and the great.

[14] May the Lord give you increase, you and your children!

[15] May you be blessed by the Lord, who made heaven and earth!

[16] The heavens are the Lord's heavens, but the earth he has given to the children of man.

[17] The dead do not praise the Lord, nor do any who go down into silence.

[18] But we will bless the Lord from this time forth and forevermore.

Praise the Lord!

Psalm 115

Now use the pattern below to write your own Psalm of worship, using your name, your struggles, and your words of praise to God. Be ready to share your Psalm with your group this week.

Not to_____[your name], O Lord, not to our church, but
to your name give glory, for the sake of your_____[Characteristic of God], and_____[Characteristic of God]!
Why should our culture say, "Where is their God?"
Our God is in the heavens; he does all that he pleases.

My idols are _____, the work of human hands.
They have_____, but do not_____;
_____, but do not_____.
They have_____, but do not_____;
_____, but do not_____.
My heart has made them and I tend to become like them;

so does my_____(family, friends,

people who follow your lead)!

O_____[your name], trust in the Lord!

He is your_____and your_____.

O our church, trust in the Lord!

He is our_____and our_____.

We who fear the Lord, trust in the Lord!

He is our_____and our_____.

The Lord has remembered us; he will bless us;

he has blessed with_____(past);

he is blessing with_____(present);

he will bless with_____(future);,

both the small and the great.

May the Lord give us increase, you and your _____

(family, friends, people who follow your lead)!

May we be blessed by the Lord, who made heaven and earth!

The_____are the Lord's_____,

but the earth he has given to the children of man.

The_____do not praise the Lord, nor do the_____.

But_____[your name] will bless the Lord,

from this time forth and forevermore.

Praise the Lord because_____!

Get Ready for Group

Write your memorized Scripture.

_____

_____

_____

_____

_____

What observations and interpretations of Scripture were most meaningful to you?

_____

_____

_____

_____

_____

Summarize your key takeaway(s) for this week.

_____

_____

_____

_____

_____

What will you tell the group about the results of your exercise this week?

_____

_____

_____

_____

How has this week helped you better understand and apply the Spiritual Growth Grid?

_____

_____

_____

_____

_____

REPENT & BELIEVE			
WHO GOD IS	WHAT GOD DID	WHO WE ARE	WHAT WE DO
KING	CALLED	CITIZENS	LISTEN & OBEY
FATHER	ADOPTED	FAMILY	LOVE & SERVE
SAVIOR	SENT	MISSIONARIES	GO & MULTIPLY

05

CREATED FOR WORSHIP

SCRIPTURE MEMORY

So that at the name of Jesus every knee should bow, in heaven and on earth and under the earth, and every tongue confess that Jesus Christ is Lord, to the glory of God the Father.

—*Philippians 2:10-11*

YOU ARE WHAT
YOU LOVE

Scripture Study

PHILIPPIANS 1:8-11

For God is my witness, how I yearn for you all with the affection of Christ Jesus. ⁹And it is my prayer that your love may abound more and more, with knowledge and all discernment, ¹⁰so that you may approve what is excellent, and so be pure and blameless for the day of Christ, ¹¹filled with the fruit of righteousness that comes through Jesus Christ, to the glory and praise of God.

Observing the Text

Describe Paul's relationship with the Philippian church.

_____

_____

_____

What is Paul praying for them?

_____

_____

Where does righteousness come from and what is the result of righteousness in our lives? (v.11)

_____

_____

_____

Interpreting the Text

What is Paul's primary concern for the Philippians: the increase of their love, or the increase of their knowledge? What relationship is Paul describing between loving and knowing?

_____

_____

_____

How will the Philippian church "approve what is excellent"?

_____

_____

_____

How does an increased love result in "the glory and praise of God"?

_____

_____

_____

Teaching

What do you want?

When you read John's gospel account, it's interesting to note the questions Jesus asks his disciples. He rarely asks them what they know or what they believe, but he often asks them what they want. What do they desire? It's the first, last, and perhaps most important question Jesus asks his disciples in the book of John.

In chapter 1, when two prospective followers begin to show interest in Jesus, he turns and asks them, "What do you seek?" Or, what do you want? In John 21, Jesus famously asks Peter three times, "Do you love me? Do you love me? Do you love me?" Jesus is asking about Peter's desires.

In both examples, when these disciples respond with what they want, Jesus simply says, "Follow me." If they seek the satisfaction of their desires, Jesus says, "you must walk with me."

We often define a disciple as a learner—those growing in their knowledge of God. Thus, knowledgeable Christians are often assumed to be the most spiritually mature, as though gaining knowledge is equated with growth. But, we can all think of a time when we've learned something new – maybe heard an insightful sermon or read something for small group – and it didn't translate into new action. Sometimes there's a gap between what we know and what we do.

Discipleship, therefore, must be about more than knowledge acquisition. When Jesus invites people to follow him, he is inviting them into a new way of living, new relationships, and new habits. Discipleship is not limited to information; it's about life-transformation. So, when we follow Jesus, we allow him to shape our hearts, forming our desires through new habits called spiritual disciplines.

As we repent and believe in the gospel and grow to love God with all of our hearts, we must recognize that we are formed far more by what we love than by what we know. That's why this volume of the Devoted study is an attempt not just to increase your intellect but primarily to stir your affections for God.

In his book You Are What You Love, James K.A. Smith argues that at the core of who we are there are affections, and those affections are shaped by our practices and habits. He argues that everything we do—spiritually or secularly—is formative in the way we view ourselves, our desires, and ultimately what we worship. "Liturgies [as he uses the word] are rituals that are loaded with an ultimate story about who we are and what we're for."[1] In last week's study, we acknowledged that the world is full of rivals to the gospel: we are prone to worship the creation, rather than the creator. Our hearts produce idols, and our culture is full of rival liturgies that promote worship of false gods.

My favorite example of this is college football. Consider the cultural practices that shape our affections for certain teams. I'm a graduate of Texas A&M—an Aggie. When you're a freshman at Texas A&M, you attend an event called Fish Camp where you learn the history of the school, the traditions, and the songs. Then you get on campus and have a new community of friends, and now *you're* part of the story. You're an Aggie. Then you go into a stadium at midnight on a Friday for Yell Practice, where you rehearse the yells, sing the songs, and put your arms around your buddies and sway. So, by the time a football game starts on a Saturday and 100,000 people are in the stadium, it's almost a religious experience—it's not just about a football game anymore. Real friendships have been formed. Meaningful traditions have shaped our affections for this team and this school. And so, when the Aggies score, there is a massive response of celebration.

Diplomas and class rings signify not only a completion of a degree but also an identification with your school long after graduation. All of these practices are formative. They shape how one views who they are and what

---

1 James K.A Smith. *You Are What You Love* (Brazos Press, April 2016), 46

they are for. Cultural liturgies shape who (or what) and how we worship.

In a world full of competing storylines and affection-stealing idols, Christian worship is vital to our discipleship. Worship services not only stir our affections for God but routinely embed us in the story of the gospel: God's creation, our fall, his redemption, and our restoration. There are liturgies of Christian worship—habits—that are formative. When we sing the gospel and read God's word together, when we pray and practice generosity together, we are allowing God to continually form in us habits that grow our love for the Father, our gratitude to the Son, and our dependence on the Holy Spirit. When Christians worship together, God meets with us and recalibrates our hearts towards him, shaping us as a community to be more and more like Christ.

So, what do you want?

And what practices, habits, and rituals are you allowing to shape your affections for the one true God?

Questions for Reflection

What is the difference between knowledge acquisition and following Jesus? What does true discipleship look like?

_____

_____

_____

What cultural practices shape your affections and desires for things other than God?

_____

_____

What elements of Christian worship most shape your love for God? In what ways are you pursuing or neglecting these practices?

_____

_____

_____

Prayer

Pray a prayer of worship, expressing your love for the Father, your gratitude to Jesus, and your dependence on the Spirit. Ask God to reveal rival
stories in your life that are robbing him of your ultimate worship. Repent
and believe in the gospel as the primary storyline that most shapes our
lives. Commit this week to make worship a priority.

SCRIPTURE MEMORY

So that at the name of_____every knee should bow, in heaven and on earth and under the earth, and every tongue_____that Jesus Christ is Lord, to the glory of God the Father.

—Philippians 2:10-11

THE JOY OF WORSHIP

Scripture Study

PSALM 84:1-2, 4, 10

¹ How lovely is your dwelling place,

O Lord of hosts!

² My soul longs, yes, faints

for the courts of the Lord;

my heart and flesh sing for joy

to the living God...

⁴ Blessed are those who dwell in your house,

ever singing your praise!...

¹⁰ For a day in your courts is better

than a thousand elsewhere.

Observing the text

Describe the emotions the psalmist expresses as he worships God.

_____

_____

_____

In what ways are the soul, heart, and body (flesh) each involved in the psalmist's response to God?

_____

_____

_____

List the names attributed to God in this Psalm.

_____

_____

_____

Interpreting the text

This psalm focuses on the joys of being in God's temple and the courts surrounding it, where God's Spirit dwelt in the midst of the nation of Israel, while also looking forward to worshiping God in his heavenly dwelling place. Why does the Psalmist so desperately desire to be in God's house? Where is the Spirit present now?

_____

_____

_____

Why are those who dwell in the house of the Lord "blessed?"

_____

_____

_____

Why are those who dwell in the house of the Lord "blessed?"

_____

_____

_____

Teaching

Before my freshman year of high school, my dad and I (Aaron) took a road trip together. We both enjoy baseball, so we drove from Houston to Chicago and saw four baseball games in three different stadiums along the way. The trip culminated with us celebrating my dad's fortieth birthday at Wrigley Field—a historic stadium on both of our sports bucket lists. Before the first pitch, my dad put his arm around my stadium seat, leaned over and said, "I couldn't imagine a better place to spend my birthday, or a better person to spend it with."

It wasn't just what we were doing that was special, it was doing it together that elevated the joy of the occasion and made for a lifelong memory.

Theologians since the Westminster Catechism (and likely before) have argued that "man's chief end is to glorify God, and to enjoy him forever." Our lives are intended to glorify—to worship—God. And not only are we created to worship him, but in doing so, we get to enjoy him and take pleasure in his presence. Christian worship, and a life marked by it, is intended to be a joyful experience.

But, what does it mean to worship?

Well, at it's most basic level, worship is the expression of reverence and adoration of something. We all worship. The question is, to what or to whom will we ascribe ultimate worship? We can worship money, sex, power, sports, and any number of false "gods." In Day 1 of this week's study we argued that you are what you love—that who (or what) we worship is often shaped by our affections. We ascribe worth to what we love most. Christian worship is thus intended to embed us in the story of God's grace, allowing his redemption and restoration to shape our affections for him and ultimately direct our worship of Him.

Christian worship is the joy-filled, whole-life response to who God is and what he has done for us in Christ.

Worship is Joy-filled

When our lives glorify God as we respond to the gospel, we in turn, enjoy him forever. Worship is intended to be a joyful experience. Certainly, there are times where other emotions are at play. We can worship even in times of grief or despair, as the Psalms clearly show us, but joy is not a temporary emotion. Joy is a fruit of the Spirit (Galatians 5:23) and an orientation of the heart to be content, confident, and hopeful—despite our ever-changing circumstances. In fact, notice how often the Psalms command us to pursue joy in God through worship:

Be glad in the Lord, and rejoice, O righteous,
and shout for joy, all you who are upright in heart.

Psalm 32:11

Shout for joy in the Lord, O you righteous!
Praise befits the upright.

Psalm 33:1

Let the nations be glad and sing for joy,
for you judge the peoples with equity
and guide the nations upon earth.

Psalm 67:4

Make a joyful noise to the Lord, all the earth!
Serve the Lord with gladness!
Come into his presence with singing.

Psalm 100:1–2

God created us to worship and, in turn, experience joy. And when the church experiences joy in worship together, it is a shared experience where our joy is multiplied. This is not only true for believers, but also for unbelievers who are present and wrestling with the claims of God as the church passionately confesses the truths of the gospel.

Worship is Whole-Life

If we are to love the Lord our God with all of our heart, our souls, our mind, and our strength, then worship must include our whole life. Our affections (heart), our spirit (soul), our intellect (mind), and our body (strength) are all involved in worshiping God. We use our minds to think about and engage the mind of God. We allow God to stir our affections—growing our heart and our love for God. Even the posture of our bodies can be engaged in our response to him. In a worship service we might stand in reverence, kneel in prayer or submission, raise our hands in praise, close our eyes in reflection, or take any number of postures that best communicate our worship.

This is why worship is about more than just the songs we sing. Although music can help shape our affections for God and give us words to express our gratitude and praise for him, it is just one element of a worship service. Prayer, the reading of God's word, giving, confession, teaching, the Lord's Supper—all of these are habits we practice that shape our hearts to worship God for the other 167 hours of the week. What we do corporately is intended to shape how we worship God individually. Romans 12:1 makes this clear:

> I appeal to you therefore, brothers, by the mercies of God, to present your bodies as a living sacrifice, holy and acceptable to God, which is your spiritual worship.

Christian worship is not a one-hour-a-week kind of experience. It must be a whole-life response to who God is and what he has done for us in Christ.

Worship is a Response

Notice, worship is a response. God is the initiator of worship, meaning that he moves toward us first. He creates. He calls. He saves. He gives grace. We hear his call, are reminded of his grace, and then we respond with worship. We recognize that God, by his Spirit, initiated our worship gathering. He drew us to respond to the gospel initially and is drawing us to worship him as a church.

Who God Is and What He Has Done

Theologian Edmund Clowney once wrote: "The gospel is a call to worship, to turn from sin and call upon the name of the Lord." Worship, therefore, is an act of repenting and believing the gospel. When we embed ourselves in the gospel storylines, reminding each other of Jesus's death and resurrection, we turn from our sin and repent. Repentance is not only turning away from an old way of living (mortification), it is turning toward God (vivification) and, in so doing, ascribing worth to the only one worthy of it.

Christian worship is our joy-filled, whole-life response to who God is and what he has done for us in Christ.

Questions for Reflection

What is something that brings you joy and—when you enjoy it—brings joy to those around you? Is there a place that comes to mind where you experience joy?

_____

_____

True Biblical worship engages our heart, soul, mind and strength. Consider the last worship service you attended. What aspects of your heart, soul, mind and strength were involved in worship? When we gather as the church to worship, is your joy in the Lord evident?

Heart (affections)

_____

Soul (spirit)

_____

Mind (intellect)

_____

Strength (body)

_____

How have you experienced worship as an act of repenting and believing the gospel?

_____

_____

_____

Prayer

Pray by reading Psalm 84 out loud to God. Express your desire to be in God's presence. With joy, voice all the reasons you are grateful for God's saving grace in Jesus. Confess any lack of joy and ask God to renew a spirit of worship within you.

SCRIPTURE MEMORY

So that at the name of Jesus every ____should bow, in heaven and on earth and under the earth, and every_____confess that Jesus Christ is Lord, to the_____of God the Father.

—*Philippians 2:10-11*

WORSHIP IS FORMATIVE

Scripture Study

HEBREWS 10:19-25

Therefore, brothers, since we have confidence to enter the holy places by the blood of Jesus, [20]by the new and living way that he opened for us through the curtain, that is, through his flesh, [21]and since we have a great priest over the house of God, [22]let us draw near with a true heart in full assurance of faith, with our hearts sprinkled clean from an evil conscience and our bodies washed with pure water. [23]Let us hold fast the confession of our hope without wavering, for he who promised is faithful. [24]And let us consider how to stir up one another to love and good works, [25]not neglecting to meet together, as is the habit of some, but encouraging one another, and all the more as you see the Day drawing near.

Observing the Text

What gives the author confidence in approaching God in worship?

_____

_____

_____

What five things are the readers challenged to do as followers of Jesus?

_____

_____

_____

Interpreting the Text

How would you summarize the main idea of this text?

_____

_____

_____

From this passage describe why believers should continue to gather together in a regular rhythm for worship.

_____

_____

_____

Teaching

Perhaps one of the greatest challenges facing the church in the West is what is known as *expressive individualism*.

You do you.

Be true to yourself.

Follow your heart.

But, in contrast, community is a foundational part of God's design for humanity. Consider these commands from the New Testament: love *one another*, bear *one another's* burdens, encourage *one another*. The New Testament actually uses the phrase "one another" 100 times in ninety-four different verses, and contains over fifty unique commands for how we are to interact together as the church. It is impossible to practice these "one another" commands as an expressive *individual*. They are communal by nature.

The writer of Hebrews suggests that one of the ways we are tempted to discount these commands is when we neglect meeting together, "as is the habit of some." Habits are formational. On Day 1 this week, we discovered that at the core of who we are, there are affections, and that those affections are shaped by certain habits. The habit of gathering together as believers for worship shapes our affections for God. When we neglect meeting together, we form other habits and in turn worship other "gods."

We must acknowledge that is possible, and beneficial, to worship God individually and independently. Worship is simply the joy-filled, whole-life response to who God is and what he has done for us in Christ. Worship is not limited to a corporate gathering.

However, the habit of corporate worship is one of the most foundational spiritual disciplines in the life of a believer. It shapes our affections for God. If we are to love God with all of our hearts, and love our neighbors as ourselves, gathering together as the church to worship in a consistent rhythm is an essential habit.

Theodore Roosevelt once said, "You may worship God anywhere, at any time, but the chances are that you will not do so unless you have first learned to worship him somewhere in some particular place, at some particular time."

When we gather as the church to worship corporately, it shapes how we worship individually. What we do together for one hour each week forms how we live out our faith the other 167 hours of the week.

Let's consider elements of a typical worship service at Clear Creek Community Church and see how they might shape our affections, grow our hearts, and call us to more faithfully follow Jesus.

Call to Worship

The Call to Worship is an invitation to gather together as believers, acknowledging the presence of God with us. The ancient Israelites often recited the Shema as a call to worship:

> *Hear O Israel, the Lord our God, the Lord is one. Love the Lord your God with all your heart and with all your soul and with all your might.*
>
> Deuteronomy 6:4-5

We often begin our services with a reading of God's word or a call-and-response to remind us that God has initiated our worship and he is present with us. The goal is to form in us a desire to meet with God and to hear from him, not only in that worship service but throughout the week.

Singing Songs of Praise

There are hundreds of references to singing in Scripture, including many commands. Not only is singing in worship an act of obedience to God but singing helps us internalize great theology. We intentionally choose songs at Clear Creek that teach us about the character of God and remind us of the gospel story. When we actively participate in singing those truths, it not only shapes our minds (by helping us remember) but also stirs our affections for God. Melody has a way of moving our souls and helping us to appropriately express our heart for God. Singing is also a rehearsal of truth. We remind each other of the truths of God's word and repeat them as corporate confessions of faith. Additionally, singing helps unite us to the church. When hundreds of people sing the same truth with one voice, it is both encouraging to other believers and compelling for unbelievers in the room.

Giving

We give together. This isn't because the church is a business or because God needs your money. Instead, we respond to God's generosity by learning together to be a generous people. We remind each other that God's economy is an alternative economy, with different values than capitalism and materialism. When we build a habit of giving, we are shaped by God's values, not ours. Our gifts back to God proclaim the gospel of God's generosity—he gave Jesus so that we could have a relationship with him. Giving, as an act of worship, then begins to form in us a generous spirit outside the four walls of the church, helping those in need and seeing the gospel message go forward. Giving is in act of worship that transforms our hearts to look more like the generous heart of God.

Prayer

Praying together in a worship service is an expression of our collective need for God and our dependence on him. It is admitting to ourselves, those around us, and to God that we need his grace, strength, wisdom, forgiveness, and provision. We learn to pray by hearing others pray. Corporate prayer not only shapes how we pray, but also grows our affections for those we pray for.

Reading Scripture

When we read Scripture as a part of worship, we are reminded again of God's presence with us and his desire to speak to us. God's word communicates his love for us, his faithfulness to us, and his promise to dwell with us. The original purpose of the letters in the New Testament was to be read aloud to the church and then applied as a community of faith. By reading Scripture in a worship service, we acknowledge God's voice as the primary voice in the room. Thus, the reading of Scripture corporately forms in us a desire to hear from him individually.

Preaching

Preaching then, is not something that happens after worship, it is an act of worship. In 2 Timothy 4:2, Paul encourages his young protégé in the faith to "preach the word.... reprove, rebuke, and exhort, with complete patience and teaching." Preaching is an essential element of worship because the church needs to be reproved, rebuked, and exhorted to apply God's truth to their lives. When we learn to interpret God's word together, we are then able to apply God's word together. The preaching element of the worship service embeds us in the gospel story, reorients our hearts away from the cultural narratives and reminds us who we are in light of who God is. Thus, when we actively participate in hearing God's word exposited, it encourages us to exposit the Scriptures on our own. When we are encouraged by the word of God, it inspires us to encourage others with the word of God.

The Lord's Supper

At the Last Supper, Jesus told his disciples to eat and drink in remembrance of him. He didn't give them a creed to recite or a song to sing, he simply served ordinary bread and wine and called them to remember. Jesus, who calls himself the bread of life, was reminding us of his presence with us, his provision for us, and his promises to us. By receiving the Lord's Supper, we are not only responding in obedience to Jesus's command but also acknowledging Jesus's provision, reminding us that every meal we eat throughout the week is a gift from God. The Lord's Supper is also a communal meal. We serve it to each other. We receive it together. This reorients us from people who are merely individualistic consumers into people who together reflect the image of God.

Benediction

The benediction is a blessing or sending, sometimes expressed with a Scripture reading, a prayer, or simply a statement of pastoral encouragement. It commissions the congregation as missionaries who are called to go and apply the truths of God's word to their everyday lives. The benediction serves as a final reminder that what God said to us in this hour is intended to shape the other 167 hours of the week.

But, here is a caution: worship is transformational only for those who participate, not those who simply spectate. Watching someone sing the truth of God's word with passion is not the same as passionately expressing your own gratitude for salvation. Listening to someone else pray is not equivalent to admitting your own need for God's provision. Every act of worship in a worship service is intended to engage the church, shaping us more and more into the body of Christ where we can truly serve, comfort, encourage, and love one another well.

Questions for Reflection

How do you see "expressive individualism" played out in the life of the local church?

_____

_____

_____

What elements of a typical worship service at Clear Creek shape your affections for God most?

_____

_____

_____

How does a worship service shape how you worship God during the other 167 hours of the week?

_____

_____

_____

Prayer

Pray the Lord's Prayer today. Pausing to express personal worship, dependence, and requests.

> Our Father in heaven,
> hallowed be your name.
> Your kingdom come,
> your will be done,
> on earth as it is in heaven.
> Give us this day our daily bread,
> and forgive us our debts,
> as we also have forgiven our debtors.
> And lead us not into temptation,
> but deliver us from evil.
> For yours is the kingdom and the power
> And the glory, forever. Amen.

WEEKLY EXERCISE

PREPARING FOR WORSHIP

Prepare yourself to worship this week. Before we gather again for corporate worship, use this exercise as a way to ready your heart for worship. Consider what habits you might incorporate in your life this week to best prepare to worship together.

DURING THE WEEK

(e.g. Confession, prayer, small group, reading a Psalm every day)

_____

_____

_____

_____

THE NIGHT BEFORE

(e.g. Get enough rest, set an alarm, pray before going to sleep)

_____

_____

_____

_____

THE DAY OF

(e.g. Fast from media/TV, engage with others as the body of Christ, arrive early, pray for your pastor)

_____

_____

_____

_____

Get Ready for Group

Write your memorized Scripture.

_____

_____

_____

_____

_____

What observations and interpretations of Scripture were most meaningful to you?

_____

_____

_____

_____

_____

Summarize your key takeaway(s) for this week.

_____

_____

_____

_____

_____

What will you tell the group about the results of your exercise this week?

_____

_____

_____

_____

_____

How has this week helped you better understand and apply the Spiritual Growth Grid?

_____

_____

_____

_____

_____

REPENT & BELIEVE			
WHO GOD IS	WHAT GOD DID	WHO WE ARE	WHAT WE DO
KING	CALLED	CITIZENS	LISTEN & OBEY
FATHER	ADOPTED	FAMILY	LOVE & SERVE
SAVIOR	SENT	MISSIONARIES	GO & MULTIPLY

06

INDICATIVES AND IMPERATIVES

SCRIPTURE MEMORY

But you are a chosen race, a royal priesthood, a holy nation, a people for his own possession, that you may proclaim the excellencies of him who called you out of darkness into his marvelous light.

—1 Peter 2:9

DAY
1

IN CHRIST

Scripture Study

1 PETER 2:9-12

But you are a chosen race, a royal priesthood, a holy nation, a people for his own possession, that you may proclaim the excellencies of him who called you out of darkness into his marvelous light. ¹⁰Once you were not a people, but now you are God's people; once you had not received mercy, but now you have received mercy.

Beloved, I urge you as sojourners and exiles to abstain from the passions of the flesh, which wage war against your soul. ¹²Keep your conduct among the Gentiles honorable, so that when they speak against you as evildoers, they may see your good deeds and glorify God on the day of visitation.

Observing the Text

Which of the sons demanded the inheritance, and what was the father's response?

_____

_____

_____

List the identity statements Peter makes about his readers. What words does he use to describe them?

_____

_____

_____

List any imperatives (commands) Peter gives in verses 11-12.

_____

_____

_____

Interpreting the Text

What is the significance of being a "chosen race," a "royal priesthood," and a "holy nation"?

_____

_____

_____

Describe what had to take place for the readers to become "God's people" (verse 10).

_____

_____

_____

Why does it matter that Peter establishes their identity before giving them any commands?

_____

_____

_____

Teaching

How do you typically complete this sentence? "I am _____."

If we're being honest, how we fill in that blank changes based on our immediate circumstances. Because you are currently reading this, you might fill in the blank with "Christian," but if you were at work you might say "accountant" or "nurse." Others might fill in the blank with "mom" or "dad." These are all identity statements. The truth is that how we fill in the blank—the primary identity we claim—is often determined by our current community or activity.

However, as we have considered the Spiritual Growth Grid, we have argued that the gospel reverses culture's view of identity. These gospel storylines describe, first and foremost, the identity of God, which drives his activity towards us. Therefore, in Christ, we are given a new identity, which determines our activity. Throughout Scripture, we see that identity informs activity.

In order to love God with all of who we are, we must first know who we are. We must know who we are in Christ.

In Paul's thirteen epistles, there are 222 references to our union with Christ.

Theologian A.W. Pink once wrote:

> The subject of spiritual union [or our identity in Christ] is the most important, the most profound, and yet the most blessed of any that is set forth in the sacred Scriptures; and yet, sad to say, there is hardly any which is now more generally neglected. The very expression "spiritual union" is unknown in the most protracted meaning as to take in only a fragment of this precious truth.[1]

Our union with Christ—our gospel identity—is one of the most important and profound doctrines in Scripture. Therefore, in order to fully repent of false idols and deep-rooted alternate identities, in order to fully believe in the gospel and live in response to it, we must have a more comprehensive view of who God says we are in Christ. Rather than taking a "fragment of this precious truth," let's consider the fullness of who God says we are in Christ.

In Christ we are:
- Dead to sin and alive to God (Romans 6:11)
- Set free from slavery to sin (Romans 8:2)
- Justified by faith (Galatians 2:16)
- Sanctified (1 Corinthians 1:2)
- A New Creation (2 Corinthians 5:17)
- Reconciled to God (2 Corinthians 5:19)
- Sons of God (Galatians 3:26)
- Blessed with every spiritual blessing (Ephesians 1:3)
- Seated in the heavenly places (Ephesians 2:6)
- Created for good works (Ephesians 2:10)
- Redeemed (Colossians 1:13-14)

---

1 A.W. Pink, *Spiritual Union and Communion* (reprinted by Sovereign Grace Publishers Inc., September 2002), 7.

- Forgiven (Ephesians 4:32)
- Encouraged (Philippians 2:1)
- Faithful saints (Ephesians 1:1)
- Complete (Colossians 2:10)

If we are to love the Lord our God with all of our heart (the primary objective of this study), we must first acknowledge that this is an activity deeply rooted in our identity. Before we consider how our union with Christ shapes our love and good deeds, let's spend time meditating on and internalizing who God says we are in Christ. Don't rush past identity in order to pursue activity. Allow God to speak to your heart and stir your affections for him by reminding you of your true identity as a follower of Jesus.

Questions for Reflection

Why is our union with Christ such an important doctrine concerning loving God with all of our heart?

_____

_____

_____

Which of the "in Christ" statements stick out to you the most? Why? Read the Scripture associated with that identity statement and copy it on the lines below.

_____

_____

_____

In repenting of false idols over the last few weeks, what are some deep-rooted identities you have held that you need to repent from?

_____

_____

_____

Prayer

Get in a posture of prayer that communicates a desire to repent and believe today. Consider beginning the prayer by holding closed fists in front of you and admitting to God the old identities you have held. Then, open your hands as a sign of releasing old identities and an openness to receive who God says you are. Before you say "Amen," spend time in silence with God and allow God to remind you of who you are in Christ.

SCRIPTURE MEMORY

But you are a_____race, a_____ priesthood, a_____nation, a people for his own possession, that you may proclaim the excellencies of him who called you out of darkness into his marvelous light.

—1 Peter 2:9

INDICATIVES EMPOWER IMPERATIVES

Scripture Study

EPHESIANS 5:1-2

Therefore be imitators of God, as beloved children. ²And walk in love, as Christ loved us and gave himself up for us, a fragrant offering and sacrifice to God.

Observing the text

What phrases does Paul use to describe his audience's identity? What imperatives (commands) does Paul give?

_____

_____

_____

What is the "therefore" there for? (In your Bible, consider the verses immediately preceding Ephesians 5:1 and the theme of the letter up to this point.)

_____

_____

_____

Interpreting the text

How does one imitate God by being a child of God and walking in love?

_____

_____

_____

What is the significance of the identity statement accompanying the command Paul gives?

_____

_____

_____

Teaching

As I (Aaron) graduated high school and prepared to go off to college, I had every intention of rebelling against God and doing my own thing. Though I had a vibrant faith throughout high school and was considered a spiritual leader by my peers, I distinctly remember deciding to have as much "fun" as I could in college, thinking I could always come back to following Jesus later in life. I remember testing the waters that summer and justifying sinful behavior.

Two weeks before classes started, a friend asked me to go to a Christian retreat intended to introduce incoming freshmen to the body of Christ on our college campus. To be honest, I saw it as an opportunity to meet people and make friends, agreeing to attend with no desire to hear from God or allow this experience to deter my rebellious intentions.

That week, the keynote speaker preached through the book of Ephesians. What I assumed would be sermons like "Five Practical Ways to Follow Jesus in College," "Seven Steps to Finding Your New Church Home," or

"Twelve Principles to Christian Dating" was instead an eye-opening, heart-piercing, verse-by-verse look at the beauty of the gospel in Ephesians. The preacher simply pointed out every *indicative* and every *imperative* in the letter.

While these grammatical terms may feel unfamiliar, the meaning behind them is fairly straightforward. When speaking in the indicative mood, the sentence makes a declaration of fact—asserting or denying something that is certain. Whereas, the imperative mood communicates a desire for something to happen, usually expressed in a command, request, or prohibition. God speaks to his people with both types of statements and recognizing the difference should impact how we read Scripture.

Indicatives define us. They are a declaration of who God is, what God has done for us in Christ, or who we are as a result, often found in identity statements. Indicatives describe *what is.*

Imperatives lead us. They command us to respond to who God is and how he relates to us, defining the expectations that God has for those in right relationship with him. Imperatives describe *what should be.*

If you read Paul's short letter to the Ephesians, it's interesting to note that the first three chapters are filled with indicatives—what God has done for us in Christ. There are very few imperatives. Rather, Paul goes to great lengths to remind the church in Ephesus that before any of us had done anything, God was already at work.

Before the foundations of the earth, God predestined us for adoption, chose us, and blessed us. If you have time this week, read Ephesians 1 and circle every time you see the phrases "in him" or "in Christ." Remember the significance of the doctrine of our union with Christ that was discussed on Day 1. Paul goes on to remind his readers that they were saved by grace through faith, not by works (2:9-10), and that they are loved with a love so deep it cannot be fully comprehended (3:17-19).

We were two days into this college retreat, and even though I had anticipated ignoring any practical advice about "staying Christian" in college, I was unprepared for what God actually wanted to do. Instead of remaining indifferent to what I was hearing, I was compelled by the beautiful description of who Jesus is and what he had done for me. By the time we started walking through Chapters 4-6, the imperatives were no longer just rules to follow or good advice, but an authentic, heartfelt response to the indicatives that spelled out the truth of what God had already done.

During one small-group session that weekend, I was challenged with this simple question: in light of the gospel, is it still more appealing to rebel against God or to submit to his will? Submission on its own was not appealing, but in light of the gospel it was the only thing that made sense to me.

That retreat redirected the trajectory of my college experience and subsequently, my life. I was motivated to live differently as a response to what God had already done for me in Christ. The indicatives empowered the imperatives.

When we train elders at Clear Creek Community Church we walk through a gospel-centered training on identity and begin with a diagram that looks like this:

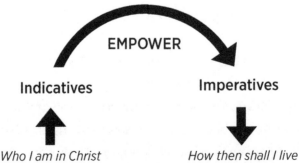

EMPOWER

Indicatives

Imperatives

Who I am in Christ

How then shall I live

Indicatives empower imperatives. Our identity always empowers our activity. This truth is found throughout the Scriptures, in both the Old and New Testaments.

Here are just a few examples:

> *I am the Lord your God [indicative], who brought you out of the land of Egypt, out of the house of slavery. You shall have no other gods before me [imperative].*
>
> Exodus 20:2-3

> *Consecrate yourselves, therefore, and be holy, [imperative], for I am the Lord your God [indicative]. Keep my statutes and do them [imperative]; I am the Lord who sanctifies you [indicative].*
>
> Leviticus 20:7-8

> *Be merciful [imperative], just as your Father is merciful [indicative].*
>
> Luke 6:36

> *Accept one another [imperative], then, just as Christ has accepted you [indicative], in order to bring praise to God.*
>
> Romans 15:7

When we read Ephesians 1-3 or consider the list of identity statements we looked at in Day 1, we should be captivated by the magnitude of God's work for us, awestruck by his grace, and filled with gratitude. When we then read the imperatives in Ephesians 4-6, or throughout the Bible, we will understand the call to live righteously. We will desire a holy life, and by his grace, we will grow to love God with all our heart, soul, mind, and strength.

Questions for Reflection

Look back at the "Who we are in Christ" identity statement that stuck out to you in yesterday's study. How does that particular indicative empower the imperatives throughout Scripture?

_____

_____

_____

Following the Spiritual Growth Grid's example, complete the following with some other indicatives and imperatives found in Scripture.

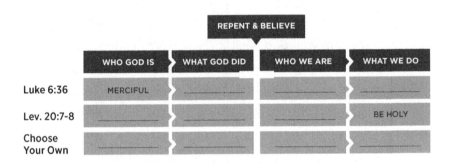

	WHO GOD IS	WHAT GOD DID	WHO WE ARE	WHAT WE DO
Luke 6:36	MERCIFUL			
Lev. 20:7-8				BE HOLY
Choose Your Own				

REPENT & BELIEVE

In light of the gospel, is it more appealing for you to rebel against God or submit to him? Are there any areas of your life where you've been rebelling and need to repent and believe in the gospel?

_____

_____

_____

Prayer

Pray through the Spiritual Growth Grid you just completed. Thank God for who he is and what he has done for you in Christ. Allow God to remind you of who you are and the identity he has called you to. Commit to live in response to that. Tell God how you plan to respond this week.

SCRIPTURE MEMORY

But you are a chosen race, a royal priesthood, a holy nation, a_____ for his own possession, that you may proclaim the_____of him who called you out of_____into his marvelous_____.

—*1 Peter 2:9*

THE GREATEST IMPERATIVE

Scripture Study

MARK 12:28-34

And one of the scribes came up and heard them disputing with one another, and seeing that [Jesus] answered them well, asked him, "Which command-ment is the most important of all?" [29] Jesus answered, "The most important is, 'Hear, O Israel: The Lord our God, the Lord is one. [30] And you shall love the Lord your God with all your heart and with all your soul and with all your mind and with all your strength.' [31] The second is this: 'You shall love your neighbor as yourself.' There is no other commandment greater than these." [32] And the scribe said to him, "You are right, Teacher. You have truly said that he is one, and there is no other besides him. [33] And to love him with all the heart and with all the understanding and with all the strength, and to love one's neighbor as oneself, is much more than all whole burnt offerings and sacrifices." [34] And when Jesus saw that he answered wisely, he said to him, "You are not far from the kingdom of God." And after that no one dared to ask him any more questions.

Observing the Text

What is the greatest commandment (imperative)?

_____

_____

_____

How does the scribe respond to Jesus's answer to his question?

_____

_____

_____

Interpreting the Text

What about the scribe's response prompted Jesus to tell him he was "not far from the Kingdom of God?"

_____

_____

_____

Why do you think that no one asked Jesus any more questions?

_____

_____

_____

Compare Mark's account (above) with Matthew's account (Matthew 22:37-40). What is unique about this account?

_____

_____

_____

Teaching

Over the course of this Devoted study we will survey every occasion of the command to "love the Lord your God with all your heart, soul, mind and strength" found in the Scriptures. We began Week 1 by memorizing the Shema from Deuteronomy 6:4-5, the original command to God's covenant people, Israel. In Week 2, we looked at Matthew's account of Jesus quoting this passage in response to the Pharisees' questions (22:37-39). Today we're examining the version found in Mark's gospel.

We've noted repeatedly that Jesus calls this the "Greatest Commandment," in other words, the greatest imperative. This week we have learned that in order to obey the imperatives of Scripture we must first understand the indicatives—the declarations of who God is and who we are.

Today we want to look at the indicatives that empower the greatest imperative. What does God say is true about who he is and who we are that might inform and empower us to love God with all of our heart, soul, mind and strength?

Let's begin by looking at all four passages side by side:

> *Hear, O Israel: The Lord our God, the Lord is one. You shall love the Lord your God with all your heart and with all your soul and with all your might.*
>
> Deuteronomy 6:4-5

> *"Teacher, which is the great commandment in the Law?" And he said to him, "You shall love the Lord your God with all your heart and with all your soul and with all your mind."*
>
> Matthew 22:36-37

Jesus answered, "The most important is, 'Hear, O Israel: The Lord our God, the Lord is one. And you shall love the Lord your God with all your heart and with all your soul and with all your mind and with all your strength.'"

Mark 12:29-30

And behold, a lawyer stood up to put him to the test, saying, "Teacher, what shall I do to inherit eternal life?" He said to him, "What is written in the Law? How do you read it?" And he answered, "You shall love the Lord your God with all your heart and with all your soul and with all your strength and with all your mind, and your neighbor as yourself."

Luke 10:25-27

Note some of the differences:

Mark and Luke use a four-fold description (heart, soul, mind, and strength) instead of the threefold description in Deuteronomy and Matthew. Commentators generally interpret this as reflecting their desire to accurately translate the Hebrew concept for "heart" which included the Greek concepts for both "heart" and "mind."

In two of the three New Testament references, Jesus quotes the command, but in Luke, the lawyer recites the same words.

In Mark, Jesus quotes the entirety of the Shema, beginning with "Hear, O Israel, the Lord our God, the Lord is one." The other two omit this opening line.

Why is there such variation? As is often the case with biblical interpretation, context is key.

Each gospel writer is including this command within a greater narrative as they tell the story of Jesus. Under the inspiration of the Holy Spirit, Matthew, Mark, Luke, and John are each writing their own accounts of the life and story of Jesus, from their own unique perspectives. Matthew (a tax-collector, government official) writes about Jesus as King. Mark (a servant of Peter) is writing about Jesus the Suffering Servant. Luke (a medical doctor and companion of Paul) is writing about Jesus as the Son of Man, his humanity. John (one of Jesus's closest friends, who witnessed his transfiguration) is writing about Jesus as the Son of God, his deity. Therefore, each writer includes the words of Jesus in the context of the greater narrative they are writing. In order to understand the imperatives, we must take into consideration the specific indicatives surrounding it.

Mark makes a clear connection between the original command and the indicative that accompanies it. He reminds the reader that in order to obey the command to love the Lord your God with all your heart, you must first remember who God is: "Hear, O Israel: The Lord our God, the Lord is one."

And in the very next passage in both Matthew and Mark, the focus turns to a discussion about the nature of Christ, his identity as both Son of David and the divine Son of God (Matthew 22:41-46 and Mark 12:35-37). Jesus seems to be making a clear connection between his identity as King and his authority to call us to obedience.

Each gospel writer clearly intends to contextualize the Greatest Command-ment amidst great indicatives. We cannot obey the imperative to love the Lord our God with all of our heart, soul, mind, and strength apart from acknowledging that God is our Lord, that he is one. To confess God as Lord is to declare his sovereign right to rule over every area of your life. To confess that He is one is to remember that he is God and we are not—that the Father, the Son, and the Holy Spirit exist in perfect community, and that he is inviting us to participate in it, by loving him with all of our heart, soul, mind, and strength.

Questions for Reflection

What stands out to you about the distinctions between the different accounts of the Shema in the gospel narratives?

_____

_____

_____

REPENT & BELIEVE

WHO GOD IS	WHAT GOD DID	WHO WE ARE	WHAT WE DO
KING	CALLED	CITIZENS	LISTEN & OBEY
FATHER	ADOPTED	FAMILY	LOVE & SERVE
SAVIOR	SENT	MISSIONARIES	GO & MULTIPLY

Work backwards through a similar grid. What indicatives empower the Greatest Imperative? Give two or three examples of how understanding who God is, what he has done, and who we are in Christ leads to obedience to this command.

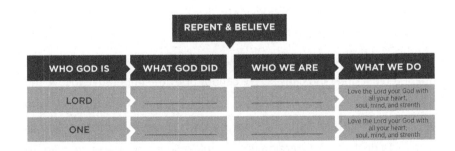

REPENT & BELIEVE

WHO GOD IS	WHAT GOD DID	WHO WE ARE	WHAT WE DO
LORD	_____	_____	Love the Lord your God with all your heart, soul, mind, and strenth
ONE	_____	_____	Love the Lord your God with all your heart, soul, mind, and strenth

What stirs your affections to love God most? Share an example of a time when you grew significantly in your love for God and what brought on that growth.

_____

_____

_____

Prayer

Pray through the Spiritual Growth Grid you created. Confess a belief in who God is and what He has done for us in Christ, and commit to love him with all your heart, soul, mind, and strength today.

WEEKLY EXERCISE

MORNING AND EVENING

Over a hundred years ago, renowned theologian and pastor Charles Spurgeon wrote a daily devotional called Morning and Evening. With a reading to begin and end each day, Spurgeon underlined the importance of abiding in Christ through meditating on Scripture.

The morning devotional for June 28 reads:

> Remember, therefore, it is not YOUR HOLD of Christ that saves you it is Christ;
> It is not YOUR JOY in Christ that saves you
> it is Christ;
> It is not even YOUR FAITH in Christ, though that be the instrument it is Christ's blood and merits;
> ... Therefore, look not so much to YOUR HAND with which you are grasping Christ,
> as to Christ;
> look not to YOUR HOPE,
>   but to Jesus, the source of your hope;
> look not to YOUR FAITH,
> but to Jesus, the author and finisher of your faith.

In light of this week's study, write a short evening devotional that expresses your own desire to abide in Christ and to love the Lord your God with all your heart. Include identity statements from this week's study, idols you've identified from previous weeks' studies, and a commitment to allow your identity in Christ to inform your activity this week.

_____

_____

_____

_____

_____

_____

_____

_____

_____

_____

_____

_____

_____

_____

This week, commit to read Spurgeon's devotional each morning and yours each evening in preparation for small group.

Get Ready for Group

Write your memorized Scripture.

_____
_____
_____
_____
_____

What observations and interpretations of Scripture were most meaningful to you?

_____
_____
_____
_____
_____

Summarize your key takeaway(s) for this week.

_____
_____
_____
_____
_____

What will you tell the group about the results of your exercise this week?

_____
_____
_____
_____
_____

How has this week helped you better understand and apply the Spiritual Growth Grid?

_____

_____

_____

_____

_____

REPENT & BELIEVE			
WHO GOD IS	WHAT GOD DID	WHO WE ARE	WHAT WE DO
KING	CALLED	CITIZENS	LISTEN & OBEY
FATHER	ADOPTED	FAMILY	LOVE & SERVE
SAVIOR	SENT	MISSIONARIES	GO & MULTIPLY

07

LOVING GOD BY LOVING MY NEIGHBOR

SCRIPTURE MEMORY

Beloved, let us love one another, for love is from God, and whoever loves has been born of God and knows God. Anyone who does not love does not know God, because God is love.

—1 John 4:7-8

DAY
1

WE GIVE THE LOVE WE RECEIVE

Scripture Study

1 JOHN 4:7-12

Beloved, let us love one another, for love is from God, and whoever loves has been born of God and knows God. ⁸ Anyone who does not love does not know God, because God is love. ⁹ In this the love of God was made manifest among us, that God sent his only Son into the world, so that we might live through him. ¹⁰ In this is love, not that we have loved God but that he loved us and sent his Son to be the propitiation for our sins. ¹¹ Beloved, if God so loved us, we also ought to love one another. ¹² No one has ever seen God; if we love one another, God abides in us and his love is perfected in us.

Observing the Text

How many times is the word love (or a variation of love) used in this text?

_____

_____

_____

List any identity statements in the passage. What does this passage say about who God is and who we are?

_____

_____

_____

What commands are given in this text?

_____

_____

_____

Interpreting the Text

What is the motivating factor for us to love one another?

_____

_____

_____

Look up a definition for the word propitiation and describe how it refines your understanding of God's love for you in Christ.

_____

_____

_____

What does it mean that God's love is "perfected" in us

_____

_____

_____

Teaching

What is most often repeated is most often the point.

In the section of Scripture we studied today, the word love is used fifteen times. John goes to great lengths not only to describe the love of God, which should stir our affections for him, but also to define the love that God calls us to. If we aim to love God with all of our hearts, then understanding this passage of Scripture is essential.

Verse 7 begins with: "Beloved, let us love one another." In the original language, this is actually only two words—*Agapetoi, agapomen*. John addresses his audience as "beloved ones" (*agapetoi*), those who are deeply loved. He establishes their identity as loved ones before giving a command. *Agapomen* simply means to love people. Those who are loved, love!

And that makes sense. When we experience love we tend to love back. When we feel loved by God and loved by people, we are more likely to be a loving person. This is God's desire for us. We may think of it this way: we give the love we receive.

But what if we have only ever experienced or received a broken version of the kind of love God intended? Ordinary love only loves because of the value someone brings to our lives. It's the kind of love my kids have for the ice cream man. They don't even know him, but they "love" him because of the value he brings to their lives. It's the kind of love some of you experienced from a parent growing up, who only loved you when you performed well or succeeded. When our experiences have taught us that love is based only on the value we bring to the table, then we spend our entire lives trying to convince people that we are successful enough, important enough, or capable enough to really be loved. And because we give love the way we received love; we tend to love those who bring value to our lives—people who are "lovable" enough. Ordinary love seeks value before it can love others.

But, 1 John 4 describes a love that goes far beyond ordinary:

> *In this is love, not that we have loved God but that he loved us and sent his Son to be the propitiation for our sins.*
>
> 1 John 4:10

It's not that we love God, but that God has loved us first. His kind of love then, determines the kind of love that we are to give. How does God love us? He sent his son to be the propitiation for our sins. The word propitiation here, refers to a sacrifice—a payment—that turns God's wrath into grace. Our sin separates us from God and deserves death, but Jesus willingly paid that debt on our behalf. He became the propitiation, the payment for our sin. That sounds like financial language, doesn't it? He purchased our right standing with God.

Jesus didn't wait until you could bring value to the table and be lovable enough. He created value in you.

Whereas ordinary love seeks value, God's kind of love *creates* value in the beloved.

Reader's Digest published a story set many years ago on the island of Oahu, about a custom for male suitors to pay a bride price to the father of the woman he wanted to marry. The bride price typically necessitated a few head of cattle. On a rare occasion, a man might pay a father as many as four cows for a wife. The bride price was a very public figure. In this culture, women would often be valued in the community by that amount for the rest of her life.

One particular man had two daughters. His younger daughter was attractive, outgoing, and personable. So, when it came time for her to marry, the father was certain he would be paid handsomely. But his older daughter, Sarita, was painfully shy and considered by most men to be rather plain and boring. The father didn't value her as anyone more than a "one-cow bride." But one day, one of the richest men on the island—a man named Lingo—came to the father and offered eight cows for Sarita. The whole village was shocked that anyone would pay that sort of price for any bride, let alone Sarita.

A few years later, Lingo rode back through this little village with an entourage of people. Everyone took notice specifically of the young woman at his side—confident, beautiful, graceful, and poised. The whole community wondered who she might be, until Lingo introduced the beauty as his wife Sarita, to the wonder of all who had known her. When questioned about her transformation, Lingo declared, "When she lived at home, she believed that she was worth nothing and lived in that reality. Now she knows that she is valued. She is worth more than any woman on the island and she lives into a new reality."

When Sarita lived with her father, she felt worthless and lived that way. But when she was loved in a way that created value, it changed everything for her.[1]

God's kind of love creates value in the beloved. When we come to faith in the gospel, we come broken and in need of grace. But the love we receive in the gospel changes both who we are (our identity) and the way we love (our activity). It changes the way we love God, how we repent and believe,

---

1 Patricia McGerr, "The Eight-Cow Wife." *Reader's Digest* (February 1988), 138-41.

how we listen and obey, how we worship God, and how we love others.

Beloved, if God so loved us, we also ought to love one another.
No one has ever seen God; if we love one another, God abides
in us and his love is perfected in us.

1 John 4:11-12

Our response to God's love isn't just to love God back, but also to extend the love we have received to the people around us. Then and only then is God's love "perfected" in us. Perfected doesn't mean you are going to love perfectly. A better translation for that word is completed. The love of God is not complete until we give the love we receive. God loved you—a sinner separated from a holy God—not just so that you would love him, but that you would love other people with the same kind of love.

Questions for Reflection

Growing up, how did you receive love? How has that shaped the way you love others?

_____

_____

_____

Describe the love of God in the gospel. How have you received love from God?

_____

_____

_____

How has understanding the gospel changed the way you love other people?

_____

_____

Prayer

Pray a prayer of thanksgiving today. Thank God the Father for sending Christ to be a propitiation for your sins. Thank Jesus for creating value in you and loving you unconditionally. Thank the Holy Spirit for revealing truth today and transforming your ability to love. Feel and experience the limitless love of God today, and ask God to allow you to love others the way he has loved you.

SCRIPTURE MEMORY

Beloved, let us_____, for love is from God, and whoever loves has been_____and knows God. Anyone who does not love does not know God, because God is love.

—*1 John 4:7-8*

LOVE YOUR
NEIGHBORS

Scripture Study

LUKE 10:25-37

And behold, a lawyer stood up to put him to the test, saying, "Teacher, what shall I do to inherit eternal life?" ²⁶He said to him, "What is written in the Law? How do you read it?" ²⁷And he answered, "You shall love the Lord your God with all your heart and with all your soul and with all your strength and with all your mind, and your neighbor as yourself." ²⁸And he said to him, "You have answered correctly; do this, and you will live."

²⁹But he, desiring to justify himself, said to Jesus, "And who is my neighbor?" ³⁰Jesus replied, "A man was going down from Jerusalem to Jericho, and he fell among robbers, who stripped him and beat him and departed, leaving him half dead. ³¹Now by chance a priest was going down that road, and when he saw him he passed by on the other side. ³²So likewise a Levite, when he came to the place and saw him, passed by on the other side. ³³But a Samaritan, as he journeyed, came to where he was, and when he saw him, he had compassion. ³⁴He went to him and bound up his wounds, pouring on oil and wine. Then he set him on his own animal and brought him to an inn and took care of him. ³⁵And the next day he took

out two denarii and gave them to the innkeeper, saying, 'Take care of him, and whatever more you spend, I will repay you when I come back.' ³⁶Which of these three, do you think, proved to be a neighbor to the man who fell among the robbers?" ³⁷He said, "The one who showed him mercy." And Jesus said to him, "You go, and do likewise."

Observing the text

What is the greatest commandment?

_____

_____

_____

What are the two questions the lawyer asks? What does the text explain as the lawyer's reason behind each of these questions?

_____

_____

_____

Interpreting the text

According to the parable, who is your neighbor?

_____

_____

_____

Is it possible to love God without also loving your neighbor?

_____

_____

_____

Compare Luke's account (above) with Matthew 22:37-39 and Mark 12:28-34. What is significant about the context of Luke?

_____

_____

_____

Teaching

What if Jesus meant that we should love our *actual* neighbors?

In Matthew 22, Mark 12, and Luke 10, the scribes and Pharisees peppered Jesus with questions, attempting (as always) to trip him up. In each account, someone asked Jesus to identify which of all the laws of God was the greatest commandment. In Matthew's gospel account, Jesus replied by quoting Deuteronomy 6:5 and Leviticus 19:18.

> *You shall love the Lord your God with all your heart and with all your soul and with all your mind. This is the great and first commandment. And a second is like it: You shall love your neighbor as yourself.* [1]

It's interesting to note that in Luke's account, Jesus requires the lawyer to answer his own question. But the answer is the same:

> *You shall love the Lord your God with all your heart and with all your soul and with all your strength and with all your mind, and*

---

1 Reminder: Commentators believe Luke and Mark use a four-fold description (heart, soul, strength, mind) instead of the threefold description in Deuteronomy 6:5 because the Greek translation of "heart" and "mind" more fully describe the Hebrew concept of "heart."

your neighbor as yourself.

Either way, Jesus tackled the question head on. The Pharisees didn't have to wonder what Jesus wanted his followers to do, and neither do we. Love God and love your neighbor. This is the same argument John made in 1 John 4—part of loving God is loving our neighbors. Simple enough, right? However, the lawyer in the Luke account had a follow-up question: Who is my neighbor?

Jesus responds with the Parable of the Good Samaritan and the application is clear: a neighbor is one who shows mercy to those whom they encounter. And yet, despite Jesus's explanation, we continue to ask the same question as the lawyer. *Who is my neighbor?*

At times, I think we hyper-spiritualize the simple command to love our neighbors. We assume that Jesus meant that we should love all people, which is certainly true. But, when we generalize his command to include all of humanity, it's easy to skim this passage without being challenged to show practical, merciful love like the Samaritan man did. The ambiguity of our well-meaning intention to love everyone leads to ambiguity in our love for our neighbors. It's possible "loving your neighbor" becomes a nice sentiment, but in reality, little life-changing love actually occurs in response.

What if, instead of having a general, all-encompassing approach to loving our neighbors, we began by loving our actual neighbors—those who live, work, and play in close proximity to where we live, work, and play? Again, Jesus combines the two commandments into one. Part of loving God with all your heart, soul, and mind is loving your neighbor, including your actual neighbors.

Clear Creek Community Church's vision of planting churches and campuses is rooted in the belief that the gospel moves along relational lines. People who have been transformed by the gospel of Jesus Christ want their friends and family to be transformed by the gospel too. What we've learned from planting campuses is that people are three times more likely to get connected at church if it is in close proximity to where they live. If more and more of Christ's people have neighbors who are unchurched people, then we have more and more potential to reach not only our friends and families, but our neighbors and their friends and their families, and not only our neighborhoods, but our entire geography.

This is a snapshot of Clear Creek Community Church in 2020: our people in our neighborhoods. Each dot represents a home of a Clear Creek family. God has strategically positioned us, with great density, to reach this specific geography.

Zooming in, this is one neighborhood. Someone from Clear Creek lives on almost every street.

What would happen if we started by loving our actual neighbors? What would it look like to love God by loving your neighbors this week?

Questions for Reflection

Describe how the gospel moved along relational lines towards you. Trace the lines back as far as you can.

_____

_____

_____

If God felt loved by you to the degree in which you loved your actual neighbors (those who live, work, and play in close proximity to where you live, work, and play), how well have you been loving God in this season of your life?

_____

_____

_____

Describe the last time you intentionally loved your neighbor.

_____

_____

_____

Prayer

Pray for your neighbors by name. Consider those who live in close proximity to you, who work in close proximity to you, and who play where you play (gym, library, local sports teams, parks, etc.). Call their names out to God and pray for them. Ask God for a chance to serve them this week and opportunities to share the gospel with them. As you see your neighbors this week, be reminded to continue to pray for them.

SCRIPTURE MEMORY

_____, let us love one another, for love is from God, and whoever loves has been born of God and_____ God. Anyone who does not love does not know God, because_____.

—1 John 4:7-8

PRESENCE OVER PERFECTION

Scripture Study

John 1:1-14

In the beginning was the Word, and the Word was with God, and the Word was God. ²He was in the beginning with God. ³All things were made through him, and without him was not any thing made that was made. ⁴In him was life, and the life was the light of men. ⁵The light shines in the darkness, and the darkness has not overcome it.

⁶There was a man sent from God, whose name was John. ⁷He came as a witness, to bear witness about the light, that all might believe through him. ⁸He was not the light, but came to bear witness about the light.

⁹The true light, which gives light to everyone, was coming into the world. ¹⁰He was in the world, and the world was made through him, yet the world did not know him. ¹¹He came to his own, and his own people did not receive him. ¹²But to all who did receive him, who believed in his name, he gave the right to become children of God, ¹³who were born, not of blood nor of the will of the flesh nor of the will of man, but of God.

¹⁴And the Word became flesh and dwelt among us, and we have seen his glory, glory as of the only Son from the Father, full of grace and truth.

Observing the Text

Who is this passage describing? List the character qualities attributed to "the Word."

_____

_____

_____

Who is given the right to become children of God?

_____

_____

_____

In verse 14, how does the Son reflect the character of the Father?

_____

_____

_____

Interpreting the Text

What is the significance of John the Baptist's role in preceding Jesus? (v. 6-8)

_____

_____

_____

Why did the world not know and receive this one sent from the Father?

_____

_____

_____

What does it mean that "the Word became flesh and dwelt among us"?

_____

_____

_____

Teaching

I (Aaron) am a perfectionist. My wife is not. I like everything to be clean and tidy, nice and neat. It's hard for me to accept that a job is done well if it doesn't meet my standard of perfection. My wife has other priorities. Hers are often better.

See, perfectionists tend to focus on the perfect product to the exclusion of the process or the people. But, my wife is a people person, not a product person.

So, when it comes to loving our neighbors, the perfectionist in me wants to do this well. I know that part of loving God with all of my heart is that I love my neighbors. I want to love people in a way that really makes a difference. I want to live generously. I want them to know the grace and truth of Jesus. But I tend to focus on the product—accomplishing the task—more than loving the person. Sometimes, planning the perfect way to love my neighbor results in a great product: a yard mowed, a generous gift, or a well-written note.

But it still misses the point.

The point of loving our neighbors isn't that we deliver great products but that we love people. What people need more than perfection is our presence.

My wife is really good at showing up. She doesn't feel obligated to have the perfect words or solve every problem. She knows that presence matters—that people feel loved when we give up our time, our energy, our resources, to be present with them. When friends are hurting, she shows up. When neighbors are outside, she shows up. When couples have a new baby, she shows up (usually with a lot of food). Presence matters.

I should know this. As a pastor, I've shown up in hospital rooms and preached funerals. I've been there for celebratory moments like weddings and graduations. I've learned over the years that people rarely remember the words I say in those moments (and as a perfectionist, I worked really hard to have the *right* words), but they do remember that I was there, just being with them in their joy or pain.

John 1:14 demonstrates clearly the value of presence:

> *And the Word became flesh and dwelt among us, and we have seen his glory, glory as of the only Son from the Father, full of grace and truth.*

Jesus was perfect, in both grace and truth. He is God. But it's his presence among his people that John is recounting first. Jesus left Heaven to come to Earth, to dwell among us, to be present.

The Message translation puts it this way: "The Word became flesh and blood, and moved into the neighborhood."

Presence matters. As you intentionally encounter your neighbors, be reminded that the product doesn't have to be perfect; it's your presence that is significant in showing God's love to our neighbors and friends. When you love God with all your heart, soul, and mind, you are willing to be present, even when you aren't perfect.

Simply put, love God by loving your neighbors this week, and don't worry about being perfect.

Have people over to your house, even when it's a mess. Cook someone a meal, even though you're not a gourmet chef. Share your faith, even though you don't have all the answers all the time. Mow a yard, build a fence, or help someone move. But remember that presence is about people, not a perfect product.

Love God, by loving your neighbor.

Questions for Reflection

Do you tend to prioritize people or projects? Presence or perfection?

_____

_____

_____

In what ways does the gospel compel us to be present with people?

_____

_____

_____

What identity statements drive us to love our neighbors like Christ loves us? Are you personally living into the identity God has called you to? How might this identity be evident in everyday life?

_____

_____

_____

Prayer

Repent of anything that stands in the way of you loving your neighbors as Christ has loved you: excuses, busyness, difficulty, or anything else. Believe that the gospel is true for you and your neighbors. Believe that your identity in Christ is to be a missionary who goes and multiplies, and a member of a family who loves and serves. Ask God to grow your affections for him and, in turn, your affections for those he has placed around you.

WEEKLY
EXERCISE

YOUR NEIGHBOR

As a part of preparing a launch team to launch new campuses, we often ask people to start by loving their actual neighbors—those who live in close proximity. We challenge people to draw out their street and five houses around them. We then ask the team to write the names of the families who live in those homes, listing the physical and spiritual needs of the people around them. It's usually a challenging and convicting exercise because most of us don't know our neighbors well enough to complete it. In order to love our neighbors, we must know our neighbors. Below is space for you to sketch a diagram of your street (or apartment complex or residential area) starting with your home. Draw/list five or six neighbors in closest proximity to you.

Name(s):

_____

Physical needs (how can I
love them this week?):

_____

Spiritual needs (how can I
pray for them this week?):

_____

Name(s):

_____

Physical needs (how can I
love them this week?):

_____

Spiritual needs (how can I
pray for them this week?):

_____

Name(s):

_____

Physical needs (how can I
love them this week?):

_____

Spiritual needs (how can I
pray for them this week?):

_____

Name(s):

_____

Physical needs (how can I
love them this week?):

_____

Spiritual needs (how can I
pray for them this week?):

_____

Name(s):

_____

Physical needs (how can I
love them this week?):

_____

Spiritual needs (how can I
pray for them this week?):

_____

Name(s):

_____

Physical needs (how can I
love them this week?):

_____

Spiritual needs (how can I
pray for them this week?):

_____

We realize that embracing Christ and the gospel is ultimately something only God can do in the hearts of people. This demands that we pray for our unchurched friends and neighbors. As we've mentioned in previous studies, your Top 5 is a list of the five people you most want to see receive the gospel of Jesus Christ. Part of living on mission with Clear Creek Community Church and loving your neighbors is developing a Top 5 and praying for them regularly—asking God to bring them to himself and use you as part of that process. Your Top 5 is also a reminder of those we should be intentionally developing authentic relationships with. List your personal Top 5 and commit to pray for them, using the prompts below. This may include neighbors who work, live, and play in close proximity to you, but it may also include family and close friends.

Who are the five people you most want to see come to saving faith in Jesus this year? This week in your small group divide into prayer partners, share your Top 5, and commit to pray for your partner's Top 5 list the following week.

YOUR TOP 5:

1. _____
2. _____
3. _____
4. _____
5. _____

PRAY THAT...

God draws them to himself (John 6:44)

They seek to know God (Acts 17:27, Deut 4:29)

They believe the Scriptures (1 Thess. 2:13, Romans 10:17)

Satan is bound from blinding them to the truth (Matt. 13:19, 2 Cor. 4:4)

The Holy Spirit works in them (John 16:8-13)

God sends someone to lead them to Christ (Matt. 9:37-38)

They believe in Christ as Savior (John 1:12, John 5:24)

They turn from sin (Acts 7:30-31, Acts 3:19)

They confess Christ as Lord (Romans 10:9-10)

They yield all to follow Christ (2 Cor. 5:15, Phil. 3:7-8)

They take root and grow in Christ (Col. 2:6-7)

Get Ready for Group

Write your memorized Scripture.

_____

_____

_____

_____

_____

What observations and interpretations of Scripture were most meaningful to you?

_____

_____

_____

_____

_____

Summarize your key takeaway(s) for this week.

_____

_____

_____

_____

_____

What will you tell the group about the results of your exercise this week?

_____

_____

_____

_____

How has this week helped you better understand and apply the Spiritual Growth Grid?

_____

_____

_____

_____

_____

REPENT & BELIEVE			
WHO GOD IS	WHAT GOD DID	WHO WE ARE	WHAT WE DO
KING	CALLED	CITIZENS	LISTEN & OBEY
FATHER	ADOPTED	FAMILY	LOVE & SERVE
SAVIOR	SENT	MISSIONARIES	GO & MULTIPLY

08

LOVING A GENEROUS GOD BY
LIVING GENEROUSLY

SCRIPTURE MEMORY

Beloved, let us love one another, for love is from God, and whoever loves has been born of God and knows God. Anyone who does not love does not know God, because God is love.

—1 John 4:7-8

THE GENEROSITY FORMULA

Scripture Study

2 CORINTHIANS 8:1-15

We want you to know, brothers, about the grace of God that has been given among the churches of Macedonia, ²for in a severe test of affliction, their abundance of joy and their extreme poverty have overflowed in a wealth of generosity on their part. ³For they gave according to their means, as I can testify, and beyond their means, of their own accord, ⁴begging us earnestly for the favor of taking part in the relief of the saints— ⁵and this, not as we expected, but they gave themselves first to the Lord and then by the will of God to us. ⁶Accordingly, we urged Titus that as he had started, so he should complete among you this act of grace. ⁷But as you excel in everything—in faith, in speech, in knowledge, in all earnestness, and in our love for you— see that you excel in this act of grace also.

⁸I say this not as a command, but to prove by the earnestness of others that your love also is genuine. ⁹For you know the grace of our Lord Jesus Christ, that though he was rich, yet for your sake he became poor, so that you by his poverty might become rich. ¹⁰And in this matter I give my judg-

ment: this benefits you, who a year ago started not only to do this work but also to desire to do it. ¹¹So now finish doing it as well, so that your readiness in desiring it may be matched by your completing it out of what you have. ¹²For if the readiness is there, it is acceptable according to what a person has, not according to what he does not have. ¹³For I do not mean that others should be eased and you burdened, but that as a matter of fairness ¹⁴your abundance at the present time should supply their need, so that their abundance may supply your need, that there may be fairness. ¹⁵As it is written, "Whoever gathered much had nothing left over, and whoever gathered little had no lack."

Observing the Text

According to verse 5, what is the motivation for the Macedonian generosity?

_____

_____

_____

In what areas of life are the Corinthians excelling? Where are they not excelling?

_____

_____

_____

Does Paul command generosity?

_____

_____

_____

Interpreting the Text

Why does Paul not command them to be generous? Instead what does he appeal to?

_____

_____

_____

To whom does Paul point as the ultimate example of generosity (vs 9)?

_____

_____

_____

Define grace according to this passage. What is the impact of Paul using economic language to define grace for the Corinthians?

_____

_____

_____

Teaching

Our Scripture memory for the week, 1 John 4:7-8, makes a shocking statement: "Whoever loves has been born of God and knows God. _Anyone who does not love does not know God._"

Why?

"Because God is love." Part of repenting and believing in the gospel is loving God, and part of loving God is loving people. And when we don't love people, John argues, we don't know God.

The passage we studied today (2 Corinthians 8:1-15) makes some equally shocking statements. Paul, in writing to the Corinthian church, challenges them to *prove* that their "love is genuine" (v. 8). Is it possible for us to prove that we love God and love people?

In this passage, Paul is writing on behalf of the church in Jerusalem, believers that have experienced not only persecution but famine, and thus are struggling financially. The Corinthian church had pledged to generously support them, to love them, but they hadn't yet followed through with their commitment. They excelled in faith, speech, and conduct—meaning they believed the right things, they said the right things, they may have acted the right way—but they weren't living generous lives as a church. So, Paul says, *prove that your love is genuine.*

How do you prove love? Paul illustrates it two ways:

1. **The Macedonian Church (2 Corinthians 8:1-5)**

> *We want you to know, brothers, about the grace of God that has been given among the* **churches of Macedonia,** *for in a severe test of affliction, their abundance of joy and their extreme poverty have overflowed in a wealth of generosity on their part. For they gave according to their means, as I can testify, and beyond their means, of their own accord, begging us earnestly for the favor of taking part in the relief of the saints— and this, not as we expected, but they gave themselves first to the Lord and then by the will of God to us.*

Notice the formula Paul gives. Their "abundance of joy" plus their "extreme poverty" has resulted in a "wealth of generosity."

JOY + POVERTY = GENEROSITY

That's not a formula we'd expect. If we are poor, how are we supposed to be generous? If we are in debt, how can we give to those in need? We assume generous people are those who have such an abundance of resources that they have enough to give a little extra away. But what if JOY + POVERTY = GENEROSITY because the Macedonians loved people and their joy in the gospel overflowed in act of generosity? What if generosity wasn't tied to their financial status but rather was motivated by the gospel?

Notice, they begged for the favor of taking part in this generous gift. They "gave themselves first to the Lord and then" to this offering. But Paul doesn't stop there. He appeals to one more example of love—the greatest example.

2. **The Gospel (2 Corinthians 8:9)**

> *For you know the grace of our Lord Jesus Christ, that though he was rich, yet for your sake he became poor, so that you by his poverty might become rich.*

Notice the financial language used by Paul: "Though he was rich"—though Jesus had every resource imaginable in heaven (wealth, time, relationships, love, holiness, etc.)—"yet for your sake, he became poor." And Paul isn't just speaking figuratively. Jesus became poor, literally.

Jesus was born in a feeding trough. He lived with the lowest of the low on the economic scale. In Luke 9:58, Jesus said "the Son of Man has nowhere to lay his head." He was essentially homeless. At the end of his life, Jesus rode into Jerusalem on a borrowed donkey, ate dinner in a borrowed room, and, when he died, was laid in a borrowed tomb. At the cross, the guards cast lots for Jesus's only possession, a robe, and in that moment, he was stripped of literally everything he owned.

Jesus became poor.

"So that you by his poverty might become rich."

Jesus loved you so much that he gave away everything so that he could give you grace, forgiveness, hope, purpose, and life. That is the gospel, the good news of Jesus. Paul is just using financial language to describe the kind of love we've been looking at throughout this entire study. God is generous.

So, what if generosity was a means for proving our love for people? What if generosity was this inevitable sign of our understanding of grace? What if it was a mark of those who truly love God with all their heart, all their mind, and all their strength?

And, what if generosity had less to do with our financial status and more to do with our understanding of the gospel of grace?

The foundation for our love for God and our love for others is the grace of Jesus Christ. Loving a generous God and loving his people means responding with a generosity of our own.

Questions for Reflection

How would you define generosity? What words come to mind when you think about truly generous people?

_____

_____

_____

How can understanding the gospel of God's grace to us change our motivation for generosity?

_____

_____

Generosity is about more than just money, but it does include our money along with all of our other resources. How can we as a group challenge each other to practice whole-life generosity this week?

_____

_____

_____

Prayer

Confess any natural reactions you have when the church talks about generosity and money. Repent of any idols that may threaten a biblical view of generosity and money. Believe the gospel. Imagine Jesus becoming poor so that you could inherit grace. Thank God for his generosity and ask him to grow your generosity towards others.

SCRIPTURE MEMORY

Beloved, let us love one another, for

_____, and whoever loves

has been born of God and knows

God. Anyone_____does

not know God, because God is love.

—1 John 4:7-8

CONTAGIOUS GENEROSITY

Scripture Study

2 CORINTHIANS 9:6-8

The point is this: whoever sows sparingly will also reap sparingly, and whoever sows bountifully will also reap bountifully. ⁷Each one must give as he has decided in his heart, not reluctantly or under compulsion, for God loves a cheerful giver. ⁸And God is able to make all grace abound to you, so that having all sufficiency in all things at all times, you may abound in every good work.

Observing the text

In your own words, explain the farming illustration Paul uses to begin this section of his letter to the Corinthians.

_____

_____

_____

According to this passage, what are the results of cheerful giving?

_____

_____

_____

How is God described in this passage? What actions does he take towards those who give generously?

_____

_____

_____

Interpreting the text

What kind of blessings is Paul referring to when he says you will "reap bountifully" and that "grace will abound to you"?

_____

_____

_____

Describe a time when you gave "reluctantly or under compulsion." Contrast that with a time when you gave "willingly and cheerfully."

_____

_____

_____

Teaching

During small group, a young kindergarten teacher asked for prayer for a fellow teacher and her husband who were recent empty nesters. They had decided to adopt one of her students and his three-year-old sister. The lives of these children had been filled with pain and struggle. This adoption would change everything for these hurting children, but it came at a great cost to this aging couple.

While the small group discussed how generous and loving this teacher and her family were, they decided to do something to help—they wanted to be generous too. So, they pooled some money together and were able to purchase a new bunk bed, mattresses, bedding, and other items to get these children settled into their new home.

The sacrifice of these adoptive parents was inspiring, and that kind of generosity begat more generosity. Generous giving is contagious.

But it's not natural.

Most of us do not give away the resources we have, unprompted. Various motivations may be at play, but our default, hard-wired response is self-preservation—hoarding resources to ensure we have enough.

That's what Paul is arguing in 2 Corinthians 8-9. The church at Corinth was holding back. They were sowing sparingly. But Paul says that in God's economy, when you are reluctant to be generous, you will "reap sparingly"—you won't experience the fullness of joy that God intends for you. However, when you rely on God and trust in his provision, when you are inspired by God's generosity towards you and the generosity of other believers, when you choose to be someone who "sows bountifully" (gives generously), then God will not only provide for your needs, but his grace will also abound. He will continue to be generous towards you, however he best sees fit.

The kind of generosity God calls us to, the kind of generosity we see taught in Scripture, is not natural—it's *super*natural. It's motivated by the grace of

God. It's his power in us changing our hearts from self-preservation mode to a dependence on God, from reluctant obligation to joyful generosity. It begins with our hearts, not our wallets.

God's intention, from the beginning, is that we would love him with all of our hearts in full devotion to him, but he knows that money often gets in the way. It's one of those idols our hearts produce that can steal our joy if we aren't careful. What if God calls us to give generously not because he needs our money, but because he wants our hearts?

Remember, God doesn't need anything from us. He has every resource at his disposal and is perfectly capable of accomplishing his will, with or without our contribution. So, giving out of obligation is worthless anyway. This is about your heart, not about your wallet.

We must repent of old ways of viewing money and believe in the gospel, turning away from reluctant obligation and being reminded of the grace we have received in Christ. God was not reluctant in his grace towards you. He gave joyfully. We are to reflect this same kind of joyful generosity to those around us. And when we do, our generosity can become contagious.

Consider this Generosity Cycle[1]:

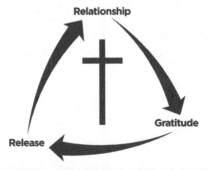

Relationship

Gratitude

Release

1 Skye Jenthani. *Whole Life Generosity Devotional: Living in Relationship, Gratitude, and Release* (Generous Church, September 2018), 90.

Imagine someone bailed you out, forgave a loan, or gave you an unexpected gift. Now imagine they said, "This is a no-strings-attached gift. But, if you feel the need to thank me, simply do for someone else—to whatever degree you can—what I've just done for you."[2] Chances are we'd do that, because that relationship led to such gratitude that we'd be willing to release any resources necessary.

Love God with all your heart. Repent and believe in the gospel.
And when we do, generosity begets more generosity.

Questions for Reflection

Give an example of the most generous gift you've ever personally been given. How did you feel when you received it?

_____

_____

_____

How would your life change if you viewed generosity as an opportunity to express gratitude?

_____

_____

_____

What thoughts/actions/beliefs do you need to repent of when it comes to money? How does the gospel change your view of generosity?

_____

_____

_____

---

2 Andy Stanley. *Starting Point Conversation Guide Revised Edition: A Conversation About Faith* (Zondervan, January 2015), 94.

Prayer

Express your gratitude towards God for the cross and resurrection. Hold your hands open, with your palms up, as a symbol of releasing any resources God may be calling you to be generous with. Ask God for opportunities to practice generous living this week, with your neighbors, co-workers, family, and friends.

SCRIPTURE MEMORY

Beloved, let us love_____, for

love_____, and whoever loves

_____of God and knows

God. Anyone who does not love_____

_____, because God is love.

—1 John 4:7-8

WHOLE-LIFE GENEROSITY

Scripture Study

ACTS 3:1-10

Now Peter and John were going up to the temple at the hour of prayer, the ninth hour. ²And a man lame from birth was being carried, whom they laid daily at the gate of the temple that is called the Beautiful Gate to ask alms of those entering the temple. ³Seeing Peter and John about to go into the temple, he asked to receive alms. ⁴And Peter directed his gaze at him, as did John, and said, "Look at us." ⁵And he fixed his attention on them, expecting to receive something from them. ⁶But Peter said, "I have no silver and gold, but what I do have I give to you. In the name of Jesus Christ of Nazareth, rise up and walk!" ⁷And he took him by the right hand and raised him up, and immediately his feet and ankles were made strong. ⁸And leaping up, he stood and began to walk, and entered the temple with them, walking and leaping and praising God. ⁹And all the people saw him walking and praising God, ¹⁰and recognized him as the one who sat at the Beautiful Gate of the temple, asking for alms. And they were filled with wonder and amazement at what had happened to him.

Observing the Text

Why were Peter and John at the temple? What were they going to do?

_____

_____

_____

How did Peter respond to the request from the man begging at the gate? What did he say and do?

_____

_____

_____

What was the response to this act of generosity, from both the man healed and the crowds around him?

_____

_____

_____

Interpreting the Text

What is the significance of Peter directing his gaze at him and touching the man?

_____

_____

_____

How were Peter and John generous with the man, despite not giving gold or silver?

_____

_____

_____

Teaching

In our culture, both inside and outside the church, we tend to limit our understanding of generosity to a financial expression. We assume that generosity is all about giving money or economic resources to others. While finances are a part of generosity, such a narrow definition falls short of the vision God has for his followers.

In Acts 3, the church was in its infancy. Peter had recently preached on Pentecost, where three thousand people came to faith and were baptized. In a city like Jerusalem, Peter and John would have been well known, and their reputations were on the rise. They had become busy men, with many responsibilities, and were on their way to the temple to worship. At the gate was a man who laid there every day, likely disheveled, begging for money, unable to work due to a lifelong paralysis. Thousands of people would have passed by this man every day, but as you can imagine, very few really saw him. Think about that: a man created in the image of God blending into the background of a bustling city, an unimportant, unseen object of little value to most who walked by.

But Peter and John saw him. Notice, Acts tells us Peter "directed his gaze" at the paralyzed man. They saw him and spoke to him. "Look at us," Peter said. Peter and John gave him the dignity of being seen and known. Then Peter told him that he carried no money, but he was willing to give what he had. "In the name of Jesus Christ of Nazareth, rise up and walk!" And the man was healed.

Notice how, even without giving money, Peter and John were generous to this man. They gave him attention. They treated him with dignity. They shared their time. They gave him restoration. And through the power of Jesus, they gave him healing.

Peter and John were simply doing what they had seen Jesus do through-out his ministry. Jesus gave himself in every way imaginable—time, attention, love, power. He even gave his life for his enemies. Jesus was incredibly generous, but a vast majority of the examples we see of Jesus's generosity had nothing to do with financial resources. Jesus, Peter, and John did not limit their definition or practice of generosity to silver and gold. Rather, their lives were defined by whole-life generosity.[1]

This is what Paul argues in 2 Corinthians 9:8. "And God is able to make all grace abound to you, so that having all sufficiency in all things at all times, you may abound in every good work." God has been generous to us in all things and has called us to be generous in every good work as well. Whole-Life Generosity may include financial resources, but it's not limited to them. It's all things. Consider all the resources God has given you: time, energy, influence, power, forgiveness, a home, a car, skills, talents. The list could go on. God has graciously given us all things, and therefore we are called to be gracious in every way—to practice whole-life generosity.

Questions for Reflection

Write your own personal definition of generosity.

_____

_____

_____

Make a list of ten resources God has graciously given you.

1. _____

2. _____

3. _____

4. _____

5. _____

1 For more on whole-life generosity read Skye Jethani's, *Whole-Life Generosity Devotional: Living in Relationship, Gratitude and Release.*

6. _____
7. _____
8. _____
9. _____
10. _____

If God is the owner of all things, and you manage the resources He has given you, how can you be generous with each of those same ten resources?

1. _____
2. _____
3. _____
4. _____
5. _____
6. _____
7. _____
8. _____
9. _____
10. _____

If part of loving a generous God is living a generous life, what lack of generosity must you repent of? What are you struggling to believe is true about God's generosity towards you?

_____

_____

_____

Prayer

Worship God as a generous giver, recognizing the ways he has blessed you, even beyond financial means. Pray over the list of resources you wrote above, asking God to grow your heart to practice whole-life generosity this week.

WEEKLY EXERCISE

GENEROSITY CHALLENGE

This week's exercise is a seven-day Generosity Challenge. For the next week, read the generosity prompts below and commit to one act of generosity every day for the next seven days. If helpful, take a picture of the prompts below with your cell phone and save it as a reference for the week. Then be ready to share your experience with your small group members over the next several meetings. Remember, generosity is contagious. Tell stories and encourage people in your group to be generous along with you.

Generosity Prompts:

1. Buy a candy bar or some other small item for a friend/coworker/neighbor. Hand it to them or place it on their desk with a note (don't make a big deal of it or expect anything in return).

2. Help in an area that you normally would not. For example, do someone else's chore at home, assist a coworker in their responsibility at work, take a neighbor's trash can back from the curb (and try to do it secretly if possible!).

3. The next time you go out to eat, change your tip. 1) If you go to a restaurant that doesn't receive tips, give a tip to the person cleaning tables. 2) If they do receive tips, double your tip (or double the bill as a tip!). Secretly (if possible), watch their reactions and thank God for the ability to do so.

4. Give something you own away. Ask the Lord to show you who could most use that item.

5. Involving our family in giving decisions is one of the wisest things we

can do. Schedule a family meeting to talk about one new thing you can do to serve others in your neighborhood or community. If you have kids, figure out a way for them to be involved.

6. Go to GlobalRichList.com. Input your income and see where you stand in comparison with the rest of the world. Ask God how this should impact your financial giving.

7. Carry a designated amount of cash in your left pocket or separate area of your purse (from $5-$50) and look for an opportunity to give it away. Keep trying every day until you can.

Get Ready for Group

Write your memorized Scripture.

_____

_____

_____

_____

_____

What observations and interpretations of Scripture were most meaningful to you?

_____

_____

_____

_____

_____

Summarize your key takeaway(s) for this week.

_____

_____

_____

_____

_____

What will you tell the group about the results of your exercise this week?

_____

_____

_____

_____

How has this week helped you better understand and apply the Spiritual Growth Grid?

_____

_____

_____

_____

_____

	REPENT & BELIEVE		
WHO GOD IS	**WHAT GOD DID**	**WHO WE ARE**	**WHAT WE DO**
KING	CALLED	CITIZENS	LISTEN & OBEY
FATHER	ADOPTED	FAMILY	LOVE & SERVE
SAVIOR	SENT	MISSIONARIES	GO & MULTIPLY

09

WHOLEHEARTED REPENTANCE

SCRIPTURE MEMORY

With my whole heart I seek you;
let me not wander from your
commandments!

—*Psalm 119:10*

WHOLEHEARTED OBEDIENCE

Scripture Study

DEUTERONOMY 30:1-10

"And when all these things come upon you, the blessing and the curse, which I have set before you, and you call them to mind among all the nations where the Lord your God has driven you, ²and return to the Lord your God, you and your children, and obey his voice in all that I command you today, with all your heart and with all your soul, ³then the Lord your God will restore your fortunes and have mercy on you, and he will gather you again from all the peoples where the Lord your God has scattered you. ⁴If your outcasts are in the uttermost parts of heaven, from there the Lord your God will gather you, and from there he will take you. ⁵And the Lord your God will bring you into the land that your fathers possessed, that you may possess it. And he will make you more prosperous and numerous than your fathers. ⁶And the Lord your God will circumcise your heart and the heart of your offspring, so that you will love the Lord your God with all your heart and with all your soul, that you may live. ⁷And the Lord your God will put all these curses on your foes and enemies who persecuted you. ⁸And you shall again obey the voice of the Lord and keep all his commandments

that I command you today. ⁹The Lord your God will make you abundantly prosperous in all the work of your hand, in the fruit of your womb and in the fruit of your cattle and in the fruit of your ground. For the Lord will again take delight in prospering you, as he took delight in your fathers, ¹⁰when you obey the voice of the Lord your God, to keep his commandments and his statutes that are written in this Book of the Law, when you turn to the Lord your God with all your heart and with all your soul.

Observing the Text

Notice the repetition of the phrase, "with all your heart and with all your soul." Underline the three instances in Deuteronomy 30:1-10. What actions are commanded to be done with all of our hearts and souls?

_____

_____

_____

In verse 2, what must one do before obeying God's voice?

_____

_____

_____

What is the promised result when Israel repents, obeys, and loves the Lord their God with all their hearts and souls?

_____

_____

_____

Interpreting the Text

According to this text, in order to love the Lord our God with all of our hearts, we must first turn back to God (repent) and wholeheartedly obey his voice. Why is the sequence important?

_____

_____

_____

Why does the writer mention a circumcision of the heart? What does that mean? Who performs this act? What is the intended result?

_____

_____

_____

Teaching

As we conclude our nine-week study focused on loving God with your whole heart, I want to remind and reorient us to the fact that doing so is primarily an act of repenting and believing in the gospel. Remember Martin Luther's famous line: "When our Lord and Master Jesus Christ said 'Repent,' he intended that the entire life of believers should be repentance." In order to experience the joyful, intimate, thrilling, love relationship with God we have described, we must repent regularly. In fact, wholehearted love for God is only possible when it begins with wholehearted repentance. Deuteronomy 30, our text for today, illustrates this well.

The book of Deuteronomy is really a sermon, or a collection of sermons, preached by Moses to the nation of Israel shortly before his death. These sermons were intended to motivate Israel to faithfully obey the commands and covenant laws that God had given his people. He reminds them of the Ten Commandments (Deuteronomy 5), and establishes the greatest commandment (Deuteronomy 6:5) to love the Lord their God with all their heart, soul, and might. And, in the chapters that follow Moses goes into great detail, illustrating how that kind of love for God should be displayed as they enter into the Promised Land. But as Moses concluded the sermon, he carefully explained both the blessings that would accompany their obedience and the curses that would result from disobedience (Deuteronomy 28).

In God's sovereignty, he knew Israel would experience both blessing and curse in their sordid history. Deuteronomy 30, then, foreshadows not only Israel's rebellion and their eventual exile, but God's consistent desire to restore them if they would repent. He outlines his hope for his people to wholeheartedly turn back, to wholeheartedly love him, and to wholeheartedly obey.

In fact, notice that the same phrase we see in the Shema (Deuteronomy 6:4-5), is repeated three times in Deuteronomy 30:

> *²and return to the Lord your God, you and your children, and obey his voice in all that I command you today,* **with all your heart and with all your soul...**

> *⁶And the Lord your God will circumcise your heart and the heart of your offspring, so that you will love the Lord your God* **with all your heart and with all your soul***, that you may live.*

> *¹⁰when you obey the voice of the Lord your God, to keep his commandments and his statutes that are written in this Book of the Law, when you turn to the Lord your God* **with all your heart and with all your soul.**

God's desire for Israel, despite their past, present, and future rebellion, was to bring them back into a covenant relationship, not only to restore them physically to the land (verses 1-5), but to restore them spiritually (verses 6-10). Foundational to this restoration is an act of wholehearted repentance.

Moses describes a circumcision of the heart (verse 6). Circumcision was always an outward sign of belonging to God's covenant people, but now God is promising a spiritual equivalent that will mark them. The evidence that one's heart had been circumcised was a wholehearted love for God that resulted in a wholehearted obedience to him.

Notice who is doing all of these actions: the Lord restores, the Lord has mercy, the Lord circumcises hearts, the Lord gathers and scatters, the Lord takes delight in His people. God is at work to turn the hearts of men back to him—wholehearted repentance that results in wholehearted obedience.

This is the same pattern we see in the gospels. Jesus began his ministry with a call to repentance:

> *Now after John was arrested, Jesus came into Galilee, proclaim-ing the gospel of God, and saying, "The time is fulfilled, and the kingdom of God is at hand; repent and believe in the gospel."*
>
> Mark 1:14-15

Access to the kingdom of God is only possible when we repent and believe in the gospel, the good news of God's work on our behalf through the person and work of Jesus. But as we have noted throughout this nine-week study, when Jesus is asked, "What must I *do* to inherit eternal life, to enter the kingdom of God?" his response is "love the Lord your God with all your heart, soul, mind and strength." Wholehearted repentance leads to wholehearted love. And, wholehearted love leads to a wholehearted obedience. Obedience reveals our love for God.

Throughout the history of God's people, he has patiently offered mercy and grace, inviting us to repent of our disobedience and return to him. However, God asks for more than a halfhearted response. God didn't bless Israel when they had one foot in and one foot out. In fact, he cursed them. Their disobedience and rebellion revealed a halfhearted repentance. The same is true for us. Our disobedience to God's commands—his perfect law—reveals a halfhearted love for God. In order to love the Lord your God with all of your heart, soul, mind, and strength, we must wholeheartedly repent.

Wholehearted repentance leads to wholehearted love. Wholehearted love leads to a wholehearted obedience.

Questions for Reflection

Are you guilty of any halfhearted responses to God's grace and mercy?

_____

_____

_____

Is there any part of your life where wholehearted repentance, whole-hearted obedience, or wholehearted love for God are not evident?

_____

_____

_____

Describe how a wholehearted repentance results in a wholehearted obedience. Describe how a halfhearted repentance results in disobedience.

_____

_____

_____

Prayer

Praise God for his unchanging character, for his mercy and grace. Confess any area of your life where disobedience to God's will has revealed areas in which you still need to repent and believe in the gospel. Commit to wholehearted repentance today that results in a wholehearted love for God and wholehearted obedience.

SCRIPTURE MEMORY

With my whole_____I seek you;

let me not wander from your

_____!

—*Psalm 119:10*

WHOLEHEARTED LOVED

Scripture Study

ROMANS 12:9-18

Let love be genuine. Abhor what is evil; hold fast to what is good. [10]Love one another with brotherly affection. Outdo one another in showing honor. [11]Do not be slothful in zeal, be fervent in spirit, serve the Lord. [12]Rejoice in hope, be patient in tribulation, be constant in prayer. [13]Contribute to the needs of the saints and seek to show hospitality.

[14]Bless those who persecute you; bless and do not curse them. [15]Rejoice with those who rejoice, weep with those who weep. [16]Live in harmony with one another. Do not be haughty, but associate with the lowly. Never be wise in your own sight. [17]Repay no one evil for evil, but give thought to do what is honorable in the sight of all. [18]If possible, so far as it depends on you, live peaceably with all.

Observing the text

If "let love be genuine" is a header for the rest of the text, how does Paul describe genuine love?

_____

_____

_____

Define "slothful in zeal" and describe how it contrasts to being "fervent in spirit" and "serving the Lord."

_____

_____

_____

What is the connection between rejoicing and weeping with others?

_____

_____

_____

Interpreting the text

What does it mean to "outdo one another in showing honor"?

_____

_____

_____

Why is humility a prerequisite to loving people the way Romans 12:9-18 describes?

_____

_____

_____

Who do you know that models genuine love well? What attributes in Romans 12:9-18 describe them?

_____

_____

Teaching

Leonardo da Vinci's portrait of the Mona Lisa is one of the most well-known paintings in the world. It hangs in the Louvre Museum in Paris, in a climate-controlled, bulletproof glass box, further protected by a rotating crew of security guards.

But a century ago this wasn't the case.

In 1911, Vincenzo Peruggia, an employee of the Louvre, came in for work at 7 a.m. like everyone else, dressed in a white smock, like everyone else, and entered the empty room where the Mona Lisa hung. Peruggia took the painting off the wall, hid the Mona Lisa under his worker's smock, and walked out of the front door. For two years, the world's most famous painting was missing.

During those two years, forgeries flooded the art world. Artists and conmen worked together to create replicas of Leonardo da Vinci's work and sold them on the black market. When the original Mona Lisa was eventually found in Italy in 1913, six different art collectors in the United States alone were shocked to discover that they had been sold forgeries.

To the untrained eye, the paintings looked genuine, but art experts know that authenticity is often verified by something much deeper than the surface. Those who studied the real Mona Lisa knew the specific type of wood on which da Vinci had painted and where specific wood grains fell.

They knew where cracks were in the varnish that could only come from aging. By comparing the forgeries to the original it became obvious to everyone which was genuine and which were fake.

In Romans 12:9, Paul compels those who follow Jesus to let their love be genuine, authentic, and sincere. The Greek word Paul used for genuine literally means, "without hypocrisy." *Hypocrisy* was originally used to describe the masks used by stage actors in ancient Greek culture. Paul knew that there was a tendency for people to put on a mask of love – appearing on the surface to be loving, but at their core, motivated by self-ishness, jealousy, or even hatred. In the ultimate act of hypocritical "love," Judas betrayed Jesus with a kiss (Luke 22:48). What appeared on the surface as an act of love was in the end a forgery.

God knows that in order for you and me to genuinely love him with all our heart, soul, mind, and strength, and to love our neighbors as ourselves (remember, our relationships with God and our neighbors are intimately connected), our love must first be genuine. It must go beyond acts of surface level love. Sincere love, rather, is a gospel-motivated love, and it is revealed by those who consistently repent and believe in the gospel.

Look at the rest of Romans 12:9-18. Paul will, in couplets, describe what this genuine love looks like:

Verse

9	Abhor what is evil	Hold fast to what is good
10	Love with a brotherly affection	Outdo one another in showing honor
11	Don't be slothful in zeal	Be fervent in spirit, serve the Lord
12	Rejoice in hope	Be patient in tribulation and constant in prayer
13	Contribute to the needs of the saints	Show hospitality
14	Bless those who persecute you	Do not curse them
15	Rejoice with those who rejoice	Weep with those who weep
16	Live in harmony	Do not be haughty
17-18	Repay no one evil for evil	Live peaceably with all

This isn't a laundry list of rules to keep. This list simply illustrates genuine love. Let's look at a few ways this requires us to consistently repent and believe in the gospel.

Repent of Evil

Paul doesn't just say to avoid evil, but rather to "abhor evil"—to detest and hate what is counter to God's character. Our goal should be to discern what is sinful and opposed to God's will in our lives and to repent of it. What breaks the heart of God in the world should break the hearts of those who love him wholeheartedly. As we turn from evil, we also "hold fast" to what is good. Those who love genuinely will repent of evil and believe in the gospel.

Repent of Selfishness

In order for love to be genuine, we must love selflessly. Paul describes this kind of love as "brotherly affection"—putting other's preferences above our own, contributing to the needs of other believers, celebrating and mourning together as a family. As the Spiritual Growth Grid reminds us, God is a Father who has adopted us as sons and daughters. Therefore, we are a family that loves and serves each other. Those who love genuinely repent of a me-first, self-centered kind of love and believe in the gospel. God has adopted us as a family, not as selfish individuals.

Repent of Laziness

In verse 11, we see that genuine love is not lazy or lacking in passion. In contrast, true love for God and his people motivates us to act (causes us to be "fervent in spirit" "serving the Lord"). One chapter earlier (Romans 12), Paul described how and why God gives spiritual gifts and called believers to use them with "zeal" and passion to serve the body. Genuine love therefore energizes our spirit to serve the Lord and his church. Those who love genuinely will repent of laziness and believe in the gospel.

Thus, in order to love God with all of our heart and love our neighbors genuinely, we must repent of any insincere, hypocritical acts of love. On the surface we may wear masks of love, but authenticity is verified by something much deeper. We love because God first loved us in Christ. Our love is a result of repenting and believing in the gospel.

Wholehearted repentance results in wholehearted love and service.

Questions for Reflection

We all have a desire to love and be loved. How has someone tangibly shown you that they love you this week? What did they do?

_____

_____

_____

In what ways do you need to repent of evil, selfishness, and/or laziness in order to love with a genuine love this week?

_____

_____

_____

Consider the Spiritual Growth Grid below.

REPENT & BELIEVE			
WHO GOD IS	WHAT GOD DID	WHO WE ARE	WHAT WE DO
KING	CALLED	CITIZENS	LISTEN & OBEY
FATHER	ADOPTED	FAMILY	LOVE & SERVE
SAVIOR	SENT	MISSIONARIES	GO & MULTIPLY

Describe how a wholehearted repentance results in those who love and serve. Describe how insincere love reveals a lack of repentance and belief in the gospel.

_____

_____

_____

Prayer

Pray for the church today. Ask God to help shape Clear Creek Community Church into a community who loves genuinely, serves passionately, and continues to lead unchurched people to repent and believe in the gospel. Pray for your small group and specifically, your navigators. Ask God to reveal how you can love and serve them well this week.

SCRIPTURE MEMORY

With my whole heart I_____;

let me not_____from your

commandments!

—*Psalm 119:10*

WHOLEHEARTED MULTIPLICATION

Scripture Study

2 CORINTHIANS 5:14-21

For the love of Christ controls us, because we have concluded this: that one has died for all, therefore all have died; 15and he died for all, that those who live might no longer live for themselves but for him who for their sake died and was raised.

16From now on, therefore, we regard no one according to the flesh. Even though we once regarded Christ according to the flesh, we regard him thus no longer. 17Therefore, if anyone is in Christ, he is a new creation. The old has passed away; behold, the new has come. 18All this is from God, who through Christ reconciled us to himself and gave us the ministry of reconciliation; 19that is, in Christ God was reconciling the world to himself, not counting their trespasses against them, and entrusting to us the message of reconciliation. 20Therefore, we are ambassadors for Christ, God making his appeal through us. We implore you on behalf of Christ, be reconciled to God. 21For our sake he made him to be sin who knew no sin, so that in him we might become the righteousness of God.

Observing the Text

What identity statements are made about those who are "in Christ"?

_____

_____

_____

What does God entrust followers of Jesus with (v. 19)?

_____

_____

_____

Interpreting the Text

What does it look like practically to be controlled by the love of Christ?

_____

_____

_____

According to verses 20-21, how is one reconciled to God?

_____

_____

_____

Teaching

For the love of Christ controls us...

Throughout this study, we have focused on the command to "love the Lord your God with all your heart, soul, mind, and strength," reiterating this week that this wholehearted love is an act rooted in repenting and believing the gospel. Ultimately, however, this command to love God is not what

LOVING GOD **WITH ALL YOUR HEART**

controls our hearts. The Shema, as foundational as it is, is not capable on its own of governing our affections, desires, or actions. 2 Corinthians 5 is clear: "the love of Christ controls us."

The good news of the gospel isn't that you have the ability on your own to love the Lord your God with all your heart, soul, mind and strength. It's that Jesus first loved you and died for you, so that *in Christ* you could put to death former ways of living, repent, and be filled with the desire to love God fully. To act in obedience, mortify sin, worship fully, live generously— all of these actions are byproducts of a wholehearted devotion to God, but the controlling force is not our obedience to a command. We are instead compelled to devotion by Jesus's love for us displayed in the gospel.

Repenting and believing is not only a conviction about a historic event but also a willingness to die to ourselves, in order to live for Christ. Repentance equals death. We put to death old ways of living in order to live as a new creation. "The old has passed away; behold, the new has come."

In Christ, we are not only associated with his death, but Paul makes it clear that we are also associated with his mission.

> *All this is from God, who through Christ reconciled us to himself and gave us the ministry of reconciliation; that is, in Christ God was reconciling the world to himself, not counting their trespasses against them, and entrusting to us the message of reconciliation. Therefore, we are ambassadors for Christ, God making his appeal through us...*
>
> 2 Corinthians 5:18-20

God is a savior who sent Jesus as a reconciler to restore the broken relationships between God and man. And God continues to send. In Christ, we have been given the ministry of reconciliation, meaning we represent God to a lost and dying world that needs to be restored. Therefore, those who are controlled by the love of Christ, those who love God with all their heart, soul, mind and strength, are missionaries that go and multiply disciples.

I remember sitting in the front row at a national conference where Bruce Wesley, our lead pastor, was talking about multiplication: about God's desire to multiply disciples, to multiply small groups, and to multiply churches. But, I remember Bruce said that few people are willing to do the hard work of multiplication because "you must die to multiply."

Bruce preached from John 12 that day, sharing Jesus's parable about a grain of wheat that falls into the earth and dies. But the seed's death isn't the end of the story. When it dies, it bears much fruit. Jesus was clearly referring to his own death. He would be the seed that would go to the cross and die, doing for us what we couldn't do for ourselves. But through his selfless, sacrificial act, we are given new life. Jesus had to die to multiply.

Jesus then applies the same principle to us: "Whoever loves his life will lose it," (John 12:25). Paul later makes the same point in the passage we studied today:

> *And [Jesus] died for all, that those who live might no longer live for themselves but for him who for their sake died and was raised.*
>
> 2 Corinthians 5:15

You must die to multiply. In order for us to be part of God's mission in the world, and see our unchurched friends come to faith in Jesus, we must die to ourselves – we must repent. And when we love God with all of our heart, soul, mind, and strength, we are willing to live for Christ and do whatever it takes to go and multiply. But it begins with repentance.
We must die to multiply.

We must die to our traditions, preferences, and comforts.

We must die to our selfish ambitions.

We must die to our insecurities and former identities.

We must die to how we view our time.

We must die to how we use our resources.

We must die to our pride or despair.

We must die to our plans, because God's plan is to make his appeal through us.

Your neighbors, your friends, and your Top 5 will hear the gospel when you die to yourself and are willing to go and multiply. When you love the Lord your God with all your heart, soul, mind, and strength, you are finally willing to love your lost neighbor as yourself.

So, be reconciled to God first. Repent and believe in the gospel, regularly. And in so doing, die to yourself so we can together, multiply disciples.

Questions for Reflection

In order to go and multiply, what are some practical ways you must first die to yourself?

_____

_____

_____

What are your greatest fears or hesitancies in sharing the gospel with your unchurched friends and neighbors?

_____

_____

_____

REPENT & BELIEVE			
WHO GOD IS	**WHAT GOD DID**	**WHO WE ARE**	**WHAT WE DO**
KING	CALLED	CITIZENS	LISTEN & OBEY
FATHER	ADOPTED	FAMILY	LOVE & SERVE
SAVIOR	SENT	MISSIONARIES	GO & MULTIPLY

Describe how a wholehearted repentance results in a willingness to go and multiply. Describe how one's refusal to share the gospel reveals a lack of repentance and belief in the gospel.

_____

_____

_____

Prayer

Repent of the areas in your life where you must die in order to go and multiply. Pray for your Top 5 by name:

1. _____

2. _____

3. _____

4. _____

5. _____

WEEKLY
EXERCISE

APPLYING THE SPIRITUAL GROWTH GRID

As we conclude this study, look back over the last 9 weeks and consider how each week has challenged you to repent and believe in the gospel. Consider each gospel storyline we referenced this week and remind yourself of God's love for you in Christ. Reflect on how that calls you to love the Lord your God with all your heart, soul, mind and strength. Be prepared to discuss these conclusions with your small group this week.

Repent & Believe

What must you repent of in order to Love the Lord your God with all your heart, soul, mind and strength?

_____

_____

_____

Listen & Obey

What does this storyline say about God's love for you in Christ?

_____

_____

_____

How do you love the Lord your God with all your heart, soul, mind, and strength as you Listen & Obey?

_____

_____

_____

Love & Serve

What does this storyline say about God's love for you in Christ?

_____

_____

_____

How do you love the Lord your God with all your heart, soul, mind, and strength as you Love & Serve?

_____

_____

_____

Go & Multiply

What does this storyline say about God's love for you in Christ?

_____

_____

_____

How do you love the Lord your God with all your heart, soul, mind, and strength as you Go & Multiply?

_____

_____

_____

Get Ready for Group

Write your memorized Scripture.

_____

_____

_____

_____

_____

What observations and interpretations of Scripture were most meaningful to you?

_____

_____

_____

_____

_____

Summarize your key takeaway(s) for this week.

_____

_____

_____

_____

_____

What will you tell the group about the results of your exercise this week?

_____

_____

_____

_____

How has this week helped you better understand and apply the Spiritual Growth Grid?

_____

_____

_____

_____

_____

REPENT & BELIEVE

WHO GOD IS	WHAT GOD DID	WHO WE ARE	WHAT WE DO
KING	CALLED	CITIZENS	LISTEN & OBEY
FATHER	ADOPTED	FAMILY	LOVE & SERVE
SAVIOR	SENT	MISSIONARIES	GO & MULTIPLY

Made in the USA
Coppell, TX
17 September 2022